Skating On Skis

Before beginning any new exercise program, check with your physician.

Skating On Skis

Dick Mansfield

Post Office Box 7067
Syracuse, NY 13261

Copyright © 1988 by Richard H. Mansfield

Design and illustrations by Bill Woodruff

Library of Congress Cataloging-in-Publication Data

Mansfield, Dick, 1940-
   Skating on skis.

   Bibliography: p.
   Includes index.
   Summary: Gives instructions for using the new skating techniques in cross-country skiing and offers guidance in equipment selection, waxing, racing, and general training.
   1. Cross-country skiing. [1. Cross-country skiing]
I. Title.
GV855.3.M37 1988   796.93   87-14563
ISBN 0-937921-37-8 (pbk.)

CONTENTS

1 What's this thing called skating?

The skier up ahead paused in the track as he looked back and saw me skating, coming up behind him. "I'm going to have to give that a try," he said as I V-skated by him. I yelled back over my shoulder as I moved on, "Try it, it's lots of fun—and easy!" I meant every word.

Remember the first time you saw ski-skating? Whether it was World Cup skiers on TV or a lycra-clad racer at a touring center, your first thought probably was, "What is that skier doing?" Then you undoubtedly noticed how fluid the movement was and how fast the person was moving. Were you tempted to follow behind, mimicking the back and forth action? Most of us were. Skating on skis is alluring when you first see it done properly. I've talked to ski skaters who train at touring centers or other public facilities—they recall how they've looked back behind them and have seen skiers of all sorts and ages taking a few tentative steps, trying to skate on skis. Unfortunately, many of these skiers have heavy skis with no-wax bottoms and short flimsy poles. Trying to skate with such gear makes it a chore leading to statements like, "I'm too weak to skate" or, "It takes too much energy."

Don't believe tales about how strenuous or demanding skating on snow is. They are misleading. Any fit individual,

Young skiers find skating easy to learn

with some help on technique and equipment, can be up and skating on skis the first time out. Skating not only adds zest to cross country skiing for racers and tourers alike, it actually takes less energy once you master the technique. You can really zip on glide-waxed skis. Kids learn skating easier than diagonal techniques while grandparents also find it fun to angle out a ski and glide. All over the snowy parts of the world, skiers from five to eighty are getting out and leaving "crow's feet" tracks across the countryside.

That's the theme of this book—skating on skis is fun and easy to learn. We'll look at the background of ski-skating, how to avoid common errors in buying equipment, how to prepare skis to skate fast, how to perform the latest skating techniques, how to train for skating, and how to give citizen racing a try. Throughout, we'll see how you can use simple tricks to learn from others and practice on your own. But, before we look closer at this phenomenon that has set the nordic world on its ear, let's understand the "language" by defining skating terms.

THE NAME GAME

There has been little coordination and lots of confusion about skating terminology. For many beginners, talking about skating is one of the most bewildering aspects of the new technique. For example, what U.S. coaches call V-1, the folks in Canada describe as the 2 skate. Yet, regardless of the variations and numerous terms, most coaches agree that there really is only one basic skating maneuver. For purposes of standardization, this book will use U.S. terms first and Canadian terminology in parentheses.

Here's how we will use skating nomenclature:

Diagonal V-Skate (Diagonal Skating)—basically a gliding herringbone used on steeper hills.

V-1 Skate (Offset)—sometimes known as double-pole V-skate, the skier poles every other skate. Used primarily for hills.

V-1 Off Timing (2 Skate)—used on flat sections with the double poling coming part way through the glide. Sometimes called "open field skate" in the U.S.

V-2 Skate (1 Skate)—poling with every skate. Used on flat sections and on shallow climbs and downhills by accomplished skiers.

Marathon Skate—the technique where one keeps a ski in the track and skates off the other ski. This is the maneuver that started the current skating boom. Let's see how.

SOMETHING OLD, SOMETHING NEW

Skating on cross country skis is new to most of us and yet the technique is far from being new. It is nearly as old as skiing itself. Early prints from Scandinavia show skiers with one shorter ski angled out. Hunters traveled great distances using a long ski and a short ski. Since they used the sidehills to their advantage with the angled ski, they developed a particular gait in their walking and were easy to identify in

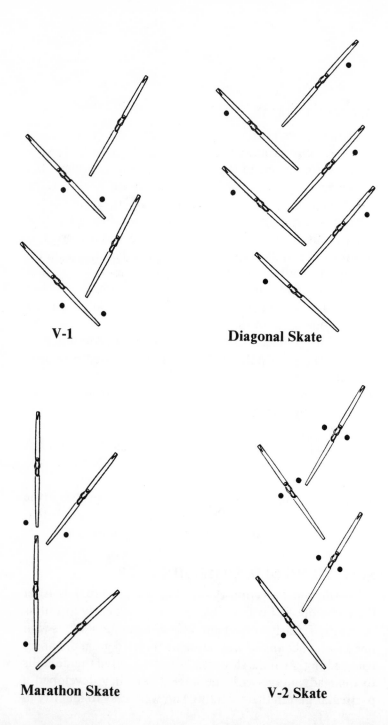

V-1

Diagonal Skate

Marathon Skate

V-2 Skate

the villages. The first overuse injuries due to skating.

So what's so new about ski-skating? Anyone visiting an alpine ski area in the last decade has seen skiers skating up to the lift line—it's the standard way to get around on the flats. Similarly, ski jumpers have skated on their long skis to move out of the runout area after completing a jump. For years, cross country skiers have known that a skating motion was a quick way to pick up speed on flat areas. Long before skating was in vogue, skiers were doing the V-skate maneuvers in short spurts. But it was the marathon skate that got the present revolution underway.

The skating revolution all began with the marathon skate

John Caldwell, former U.S. Ski Team coach, noted in a *Skiing* article that East German Gerhard Grimmer resorted to a marathon skate technique in the 1971 Holmenkollen 50K race after his wax failed; while others were rewaxing and slipping, he skated the race and stunned the field when he won by several minutes. Two years later, American skiers Bill Koch, Tim Caldwell, and Tom Siebels skated the open section of the World Junior relay in front of an audience of bemused Russians wondering what had gotten into the young Yanks.

Pauli Siitonen, a Finnish marathon skier, has been credited with the modern development of skating. In many Worldloppet races in the 1970's, he used an angled ski to propel himself as he glided down the track. Other long distance skiers copied him and thus was born the technique to become known in Europe as the "Siitonen Step" or in North America, as the marathon skate.

At first, skating was an anomaly, a method to be used in special situations such as when your kick wax rubbed off or when you misjudged the wax altogether. Racers soon found that skating was faster than diagonal stride or double poling in flatter sections of long races, in spite of the conditions.

Bill Koch, the same American skier who triggered the cross country skiing boom in the United States after his silver medal at the 1976 Olympics, sent shock waves through the international racing community when he began to pile up victories with his marathon skating. His success sent racers scrambling to learn the technique and changed the racing scene forever.

Koch picked up the technique while skiing a 30K race on a frozen river in Sweden after the 1980 Olympics. Bjorne Risby, a Swedish racer who had started behind Koch, used the marathon skate to advantage and passed Koch. Koch followed, mimicking the skating technique, and by the end of the race, had learned to marathon skate. The next year,

Koch used skating effectively on the Worldloppet marathon series and then came home to set (on a frozen pond in Vermont) world speed records for 30K and 50K. Koch, coupling skating with his great skiing skills, had the drop on the racing community and used it to win the 1982 World Cup. It was the first time (and perhaps the last) that a North American had won the World Cup in cross country skiing.

The word was out—skating was the fastest way to travel on cross country skis. The revolution was on. At first, racers used kick wax to run the uphills and marathon skated on the flats. Soon, kick wax was abandoned altogether as skiers used the marathon skate on the whole course. At the 1984 Sarajevo Olympics, most skiers marathon skated, some much better than others. The next natural evolvement would be to V-skate, to skate off both legs.

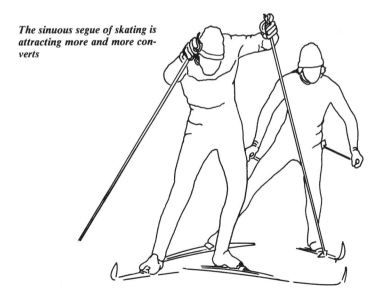

The sinuous segue of skating is attracting more and more converts

The skating movement took a giant leap forward in April 1984 in a small mining town in Sweden called Kiruna, one of the stops on the Polar Cup race series. Two Norwegians, Ove Aunli and Anette Boe, glide-waxed their skis and marathon skated to decisive victories. Aunli won the men's race by 41 seconds while Boe took the women's by nearly two minutes. It was a breakthrough, the first time that marathon skating had been used throughout a hilly race course. The next day, the top six men in the 30K had glide wax with Swedish ace Gunde Svan in seventh place the first finisher with kick wax. It was obvious that skating was the fastest way to move on cross country skis and most skiers spent the summer readying for a season of skating.

What a controversial season it was. Skating had stirred up a hornet's nest of controversy in the international racing community. The cool reception was a lot like that once reserved for fiberglass and waxless skis. Opponents, most of them Scandinavian and Soviet, fought to retain their "bread and butter" traditional techniques and to ban skating even though all top performers were using it whenever possible. Their delegates to the International Ski Federation (FIS) were opposed by a group led by U.S. and Canadian members who argued that skating was a natural development of the sport. Canadian delegate Bjorger Pettersen, in a *MacLean's* article, explained, "Norway and Sweden were against it. They had the longest tradition in the classic technique. And the Soviets were against accepting a change they felt that they could not keep up with." The wrangling went on. Snow fences were erected to narrow some sections of Scandinavian courses while in one race in Sweden, local militia were used to make large snowbanks on both sides of the track to prevent skating. Helicopters were even used in some European races to patrol against unauthorized skating. But the trend was clear. At the 1985 World Championships, the skiers voted with their feet. Everyone skated.

At the same time, there was concern among ski area operators that skating would ruin the trails and drive traditional skiers away. But, after a season or two of hassle, the whole issue of skating has settled down, both on the racing scene as well as at most ski centers. The FIS voted to divide competition into classical and skating categories. Now, most race series, whether for Juniors, Seniors, or Masters, follow this format. Ski area operators have designated certain trails for skating or have packed one side of the trail for skaters. What was once so controversial has become a non-issue.

In the meantime, what the Norwegian hunters started long ago has really caught on. Skis are shorter, poles are longer, and the sinuous segue of skating is attracting more and more converts. The reason is simple. There's no need to fiddle with wax or to master complicated techniques—you can be out the ski shop door and cruising in the first hour. Skating frees you from set tracks and allows you to fly across the snow. Let's find out how.

2 Learning to skate on skis

A skier friend of mine, nearly 70 years old, was determined to learn to skate. He read every article he could find on the subject and went so far as to buy his wife a VCR for Christmas, and give it to her early so that he could study a skating video. Once snow came, he was out on the trails determined to try all that he had been reading about. He had done his preparation and was looking pretty good the first time I saw him out V-skating.

Later in the season, as we talked, he expressed some frustration about not progressing faster. Then he went to Finland for the World Masters races, and I didn't hear from him for months until he called one evening, all excited about his skating. Things had clicked into place for him. I asked him what he had learned that helped make the improvements. "I knew I needed to have better balance," he explained, "but it wasn't until I had a good skier watch me that I found out that I was riding a flat ski too long on the hills, that I needed to edge and push sooner. It made all the difference in the world."

My friend did his homework and it paid off. Before he ever bent over to snap his boots in place, he knew the basics of skating and how he wanted to look on skis. He was ready physically and mentally. He also got some expert help to get

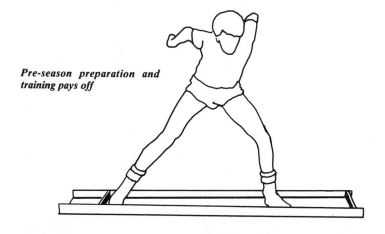

Pre-season preparation and training pays off

him over some flat spots in the learning curve. Masters skiers in his age group had better watch out, he's raring to go.

In flight school, students are asked to know procedures by heart before ever stepping into a plane. I recall the hours spent memorizing the location of dials and controls in Navy jets so to be able to pass a "blindfold cockpit check," the first step to getting into the air. Rehearsal works as well for skiing as it does for flying. Many top skiers use imagery to actually ski a race mentally beforehand: recreational skiers can use the same visualization technique to lock in the basics. Whether it's improving balance by standing on one foot in the living room with eyes closed, or training on a slideboard in the basement, there are a lot of things that we can do while we wait for snow. But before you imagine yourself skating quickly and lightly across a field of packed powder with the fluid moves of a racer, it probably will help to know some of the basics that will get you upright and moving along. Preparation—that's where this book comes in. Learn the basics, the theory, and then, like my friend, get some help to refine the techniques.

There are many ways to learn how to skate on skis. Because skating can be taught by most good skiers, you might get someone to help you get started. You might take a lesson from a certified instructor and find out the right way to balance on a ski. Or you could get video-taped and have a coach or friend critique you. Learning to skate is easy when you do a little preparation and get a little help.

But beware, it is easy to get hung up on the technical explanations and the terminology of skiing. One skier I know calls it "paralysis by analysis." Sometimes we go into intricate detail about skating techniques when all we really want to say is, "Step out on to an angled ski and let it glide a little, then step in the other direction." As anyone who skates on skis can tell you, skating is not only pretty simple to learn, it is lots of fun to do. That's why new skiers and kids pick it up more easily than traditional techniques. With all of that in mind, this book will try to keep the explanations of skating easy to understand.

Jack Lufkin, former U.S. Olympic skier, has a relaxed view of skating. "Skating is more similar to diagonal stride than it is different," he says. "The key to both is balance and efficient weight transfer."

Weight transfer and balance. Pick up any article on ski technique and you'll see those terms. What works for the slalom skier edging in toward a pole is just as vital to the nordic skier learning to skate on skinny skis. If you have years of alpine skiing experience, you'll find that weight transfer and balancing on a flat ski come easily. On the other hand, if most of your skiing has been walking on a pair of no-wax cross country skis, you'll notice that it takes a few tries to get comfortable about skating. In either case, the key is to relax and be loose. Lufkin puts it like this, "Let the body do it naturally, don't overthink."

GETTING STARTED

The one basic skating leg action common to all variations of the skating technique is this: you step out on a ski and keep your momentum going with your poles, then bring your non-skating leg in, and step out on the other leg. It all comes down to those familiar terms—weight transfer and balance on a flat ski. Anyone who has ice-skated or skated on alpine skis will recognize the rhythmic body shifts at once. After gliding on the ski, you edge it a bit as the speed slows and push off to transfer your weight on to the other ski. Weight transfer and balance on a flat ski— sound familiar?

One of the best ways to get started with ski skating is to try it without ski poles. Start the first practice on an open area that is well-packed and which has a shallow slope nearby. We will start on the flat and then skate down the slight hill later on. Here we go.

Start by spreading your skis into a slight open position, like a herringbone, and edging your left ski slightly, step on to the angled right ski. Balance on the right ski as it moves and then step back on to the left ski. Don't worry about a lot of glide at first, stay loose and get comfortable shifting weight from ski to ski. Try for a thrusting action that gets your upper body out over the leg. As you glide on a flat ski, the hips should be forward and your chin should be right over the gliding leg. Imagine that you have a crease in your ski pants. You should be able to look right down the crease from the knee to the ski.

Just as a diagonal stride, body position is one of the keys to success. You want to aim for a relaxed position between sitting back too far on your haunches and crouching too far forward. The goal in skating is to get up and forward, in front of the center of gravity, so that you can take advantage of the momentum that you've already got going. Ski coach

Dick Taylor uses the analogy of body surfing, likening the correct body position to "riding the wave." You'll feel uncomfortable with an upright forward position at first—it requires good balance. Once you get it down, it's like catching that wave, things feel right and you start to get a feeling of how easy skating can be.

There are a number of ways to move faster. First, before you step out on to a ski, turn your body in the direction the ski will be traveling. The body should follow the eyes—look in the direction you'll be gliding. Bring your recovery leg (the ski that will skate next) in close to your glide leg just before you start your next glide. Transfer your weight so that your hip is forward (racers talk about "high hips") and your chin is right over your glide leg. Some instructors call this the "TOE-KNEE-NOSE" lineup, or if you prefer, Tony Knows.

The glide phase is the time to really work on keeping the skating ski flat on the snow. As the glide ends, transfer your weight by rolling on the inside edge of the ski and pushing. At the same time, thrust your leg out with energy and get the knee out over the other ski. Keep it fluid, the gliding segment on one leg should start just before the thrusting phase ends on the other.

In spite of all these directions, relax as you learn to skate better. Remember the "paralysis by analysis" saying, and work on developing an easy back and forth movement. Some skiers actually hum to themselves as they skate, just to keep loose and to develop a smooth rhythm.

Now, still without ski poles, use a shallow hill to practice weight shifts and balance. Take some time and just work on shifting weight from ski to ski as you work down the hill. The tendency is to cut off the glide by bringing the other ski to the snow, just like in the diagonal stride. Be patient and work on gliding on one ski. Try lifting one ski and gliding as long as possible, then doing the same with the other foot, to help work on balance. Remember to look in the direction

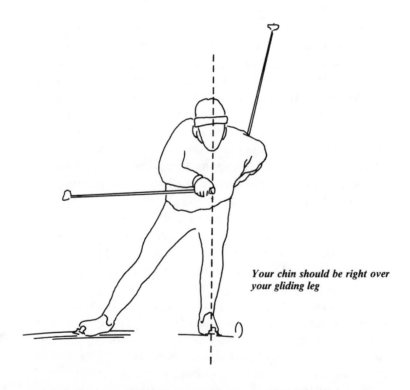

Your chin should be right over your gliding leg

you are skating and to keep the ski flat. See how long you can skate on one ski before pushing off to the other. (You will probably have noticed how long a good skier can go on one skate—it takes practice.) Mark off a section of the gentle slope and then count the number of skate strides you use to cover the distance. Then see if you can cut down the number it takes.

Here are some tips to help improve skating without poles:

1. Don't rush, ride the glide.
2. Work on developing a quick leg push coming from the quick bending and straightening of the hip, knees, and upper body.
3. Use your arms and body as if you were double poling.
4. Bring your boot in to the ankle of the gliding leg just prior to the next skate. Some coaches call this "clicking your heels."
5. Put the gliding ski down on the snow with your toes down to help transfer your weight to a flat ski smoothly.
6. Remember, an edged ski is a slow ski—work at keeping your skis flat. Some skiers place the glide ski down with the outside edge touching first to insure a flat ski.

Skiing without poles is not just for beginners. Many a top racer has been spotted at glacier training sites working on technique sans poles. During races, elite skiers like to tuck their poles under their arms and cruise up and down hill without poling. If it's good enough for them, it sure can help us. But now, let's see how the poles can add more power to ski skating. First we need to develop a good double poling action.

DOUBLE POLING

Beginners tend to use ski poles as outriggers to maintain balance instead of for propulsion. But, for recreational skiers as well as racers, double poling is a technique that can be used a lot, especially on slight downhills where you get going a little too fast for striding or skating, or when you want a little change of pace. It is an efficient method for beginners as well as elite racers. To double pole, simply push off with both poles at once and glide along, then do it again. Since most of us have not used the poles for power before, you may find the technique tiring until your upper body gets

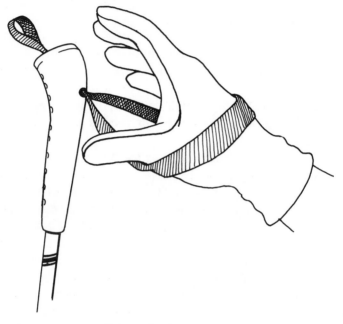

*Put your hand up through the
strap on the ski pole*

in shape. But, it doesn't take a gorilla-like physique to do a
good double pole any more than it does to skate. Lithe
junior skiers fly down the track while double-poling.
They've learned that the trick to the technique is to lock the
arms and use the whole upper body for propulsion. Here are
the basics of this vital component of ski skating.

The double pole cycle has two phases: first, a propulsion
phase that begins with the pole plant and ends as the ski pole
tips come out of the snow on the backswing; and second, a

free glide phase. It all starts with the pole plant. Reach out and up with the arms, like a diver starting off a board. You should feel as if you would fall face forward on to the snow if the poles were removed. In other words, forget just reaching out tentatively with the arms. You want to reach up and then let your body collapse on the poles to use body weight and gravity to propel you along down the track. (Finally, a use for body weight!) Power in the double pole comes from the whole upper body, the stomach, the front hip, the arm and shoulder muscles.

Begin on a level area which either has tracks set or that is packed down. First lining up your skis parallel, bend forward slightly and reach ahead with arms bent a little more than 90 degrees (this should line your forearm up nearly parallel to the ski poles) and with the pole tips angled backwards a bit, plant the poles in close to your feet. Rock forward—your weight should be on your toes and your hips out over your feet, and get your stomach into it. Begin poling with a quick contraction of the stomach muscles to bend your upper body, getting your weight out over the poles. Keep the arms bent and rigid—remember, you are using the arms basically as a way to transfer power from your stomach and back. At first, you will be pulling against the ski pole straps, then pushing as you move between the poles on the follow-through. Use your whole upper body: the trunk muscles, then the shoulders, finally the arms. The poles and the trunk should be brought down in one continuous motion. Continue to push your arms backwards, and you'll end up with your body bent forward about 90 degrees at the waist, arms outstretched backwards. Relax and glide—you've earned it. Then reach forward and do it again. Do not hold back, get your hips forward and collapse fully on the poles. Your hands should pass by your body at about knee level. (Note: There will be less bending of the torso with V-skating and your hands won't pass quite so

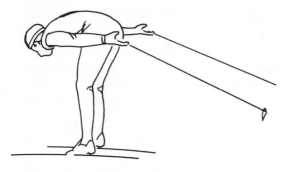

Follow through and glide

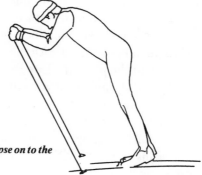

Let your body collapse on to the poles

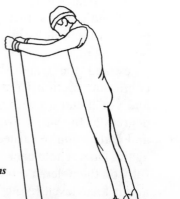

Reach up and out with the arms

low—there's not time for a full-blown double pole cycle when skating.)

The faster you pole, the quicker you'll go. Watch other skiers—advanced racers use the upper torso to get a lot of power out of the double pole technique. Double poling, since it involves the large muscle groups of the abdomen and back, is not as tiring as it might look. Once you have a set of stiff ski poles of the proper length, you'll be surprised at how fast you can go on glide-waxed skis. Combining double poling with V-skating is even faster, and once learned, is easy to do for kilometers at a time. Here's how.

V-SKATING (DOUBLE-POLE ON ONE SIDE)

If you watch a top level ski race, you'll see elite racers literally flying along the course, skating right up the hills. One of the primary techniques that provides the power and speed is the double-pole V-skate, called V-1 in the U.S. For now, instead of worrying about terminology, let's consider it as a "generic" V-skate which combines the double pole and the skate. It calls for a double poling movement with every other skate and is the most widely used type of skating today for recreational skiers. Later, we will look at some of the variations of the technique.

We know how to skate without poles and how to double pole without skating, now we can combine them to get the double-pole V-skate. You will sometimes hear the terms, "strong side" and "weak side" to describe the technique. The strong side is the skate used with poling, the weak side involves only a skating movement. In other words, you pole on one side and you just skate, without poling, on the other side. But, make a pledge to yourself right now, since we all have a stronger or preferred side, to periodically alternate the side you pole on. This will help you skate long distances later on.

We can start by poling on to the right ski. Since we've

covered all the basics, you can do it without a lot of analysis. Start a double pole to the right and at the same time, edge and push off the left ski. You turned your body toward the glide ski, right? That aligned the double pole in that direction so that you were gliding on a flat ski. Good.

As the poling push is finishing, edge the gliding right ski and, just as before without poles, skate on to the left ski. Remember, poles or not, we're looking for a strong leg push by quickly bending and extending the leg joints.

Now pole back to the right side. Bend quickly and thrust outward with the hip as you push off the edged ski, reaching out with the poles in the same motion. In skating, generally you don't get quite as far up and out on the poles as you might in traditional double poling—too much weight forward on the skating ski makes it awkward to push off with. (Remember, you're riding that wave of momentum—not too far forward, not too far back.) The pole plant is usually just before you put your weight on the glide ski—it feels like you are using the poles to pull your body up and on to the ski. Take your time and ride the glide on both sides. As you will hear more than once, a flat ski is a fast ski.

The timing of the push from the skating ski is something you will learn as you skate. There's no pat answer. Here on the flats, wait until the glide starts to die and roll up on the inside edge of the skating ski to push. When you are climbing, you'll start thrusting much sooner in the glide. Make edging and pushoff natural, keeping your knees flexed, and don't be afraid to use the ankle. When poling on the strong side, lean forward and use that upper body. Before long, once you get the rhythm down, you should be able to move easily on the flats. Keep it quick and light.

Notice what's happening with your poles. If you are poling on the right side, you'll see that your left pole is angled out somewhat—to keep it away from that angled left ski. The right pole is more the power pole and will be planted in close to the foot and be more vertical. This pole placement is natural and will become more noticeable when we climb some hills.

If you don't make a full commitment to the ski you are gliding on, it is easy to lose momentum and get hung up, straddling your skis. If things get a little uncoordinated, switch to skating without poles for a while, then try another series of double-pole skates. Accomplished skaters try for a good strong skate on both sides, with or without poles. In fact, the amount of glide one gets off the non-poling side is a hallmark of a good skater. Beginners may have to settle for a little ankle push and then have to pole again at once — more accomplished skiers thrust out with the whole upper body and get a good resting glide before the next poling movement.

Here are some tips that might improve your V-skating:
- Ski behind a good skier, mimicking the technique. Try to match the skate strokes.
- From time to time, skate without poles again to work on the basics.
- Try gliding from one side of a trail to the other with a series of double poles on each side.
- Switch poling sides every five repetitions or so to learn to go both ways from the start.

- Practice when there is an inch or so of new snow on the base. Compare your tracks with those of another skier. Who can glide the farthest before edging?

Most importantly, learn to relax while skating. Remember learning to drive? Gripping the wheel and straining to keep that car pointed between the guardrails and the centerline? Now driving is natural. Likewise, we want to be able to skate down the trail, cruising along in overdrive, without a lot of mental stress. Skating, like diagonal stride, is a continual rhythmic action—not distinct steps of "Now I glide, now I edge, now I push off, now I transfer weight." Don't over-analyze your V-skating. Get out and skate to get the basics down so that you can learn to skate naturally, without a lot of conscious effort.

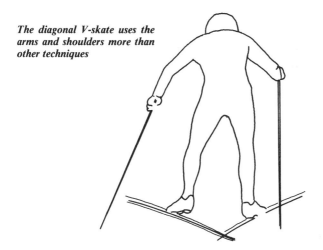

The diagonal V-skate uses the arms and shoulders more than other techniques

DIAGONAL V-SKATE

One of the least taxing skating methods is the diagonal V-skate, also called a skating herringbone or skating diagonal stride. This is the skating step to use when you are tired in the upper body or if you are tackling a steep uphill section. The arms are used in a diagonal action, just like a herringbone or diagonal stride. You'll use your arms and shoulders more than in other skating techniques.

Let's begin with a slight uphill section and learn to climb that first. Start a herringbone, angling the right ski out and pushing with your opposite pole, place your weight on the right ski. Then, edge the right ski to push off as you pole back on to the left ski. The hands should be wider than when double poling and the poles planted behind the ski just as in the herringbone. During climbs, you won't get as much glide so don't force a flat ski with this technique; make a definite weight transfer to the skating ski and as the glide slows, pole and skate off with the opposite ski. The key is to have the skating ski moving before you set it on the snow. As you pole on the opposite side, make a complete weight shift to that side.

Don't force a glide on a steep section, take what you can get. You'll probably have to edge the ski and push off almost at once but keep the tempo quick and try and be light on your skis. Even World Cup skiers use diagonal skating on steep climbs, literally dancing their way, hopping from side to side, up the hill. It is a handy way to climb terrain too steep to double-pole V-skate. If you run out of steam, switch to a herringbone and then transition back to a diagonal skate near the top. For many who skate, the diagonal skate will be the technique that they find easiest, the technique they fall back on when they are tired. Keep it in mind, it's a good method to use when you start bogging down on the tougher climbs.

*Weight transfer and balance —
the keys to skating on skis*

We've looked at the basic skating techniques—learning to skate without poles, double poling, V-1, and diagonal skating. A later chapter will cover marathon skating and several variations of V-skating. We started by discussing the two keys to skating, weight transfer and balancing on a flat ski. Get those two principles down cold and you're well on your way to mastering skating on skis.

3 Equipment for skating

Skating brings a whole new group of performance-minded persons to the sport of cross country skiing. Some are runners, bikers, and canoeists looking for a winter sport and intrigued by the speed and grace of skating. A growing number are alpine skiers who, having skated up to lift lines for years, want to give this new technique a try. They find that it's an easy transition. Parents who have kids skating in Bill Koch league or Jackrabbit league races are lured to the technique that their sons and daughters have mastered so easily. Perhaps the largest number of new skaters are those skiers who have been cross country skiing for many winters and, having read about and seen skating, decide to give it a try. If skating is what you're going to be doing most of the time on skis, you should know what to look for in equipment.

In an article in *Nordic West* magazine, skiing authority Jonathon Wiesel wrote that if you listened to the statements of coaches, journalists, and advertisers, "you'd have to expect that by 1990 most nordic skiers will be tearing along the trails dressed in single-piece suits in 6 contrasting hues; ... Any self-respecting skier will own at least 2 kinds of skis (preferably color-coordinated with the outfit of the day.)"

It's true that skating has spawned a whole array of glitzy

Skating has spawned a whole array of glitzy ski apparel

ski apparel and equipment that rivals any seen on the downhill slopes. In place of pictures of the staid laminated cross country skis that many of us began with, iridescent skating skis now adorn the pages of nordic magazines. Multi-hued lycra suits replace knickers and turtlenecks on many cross country skiers. It seems that skating has turned cross country skiing into a flashy, high-tech sport which can no longer be called inexpensive. But has it really?

Before rushing out to buy the latest integrated skating package, here are some things to consider:

1. You can skate on virtually any pair of waxable cross country skis, some more easily than others. People have been doing it for years.
2. Don't try to skate on no-wax skis, it is too much work.
3. Traditional skis are not designed to handle the torsional stress and wear of skating. They may not hold up well.
4. Skating is quite easy and lots of fun in some snow conditions. It is impossible in others.
5. Many skiers love cross country skiing for the variety it allows. They'll want to do more than just skate. Track skiing and back-country touring are better suited to traditional techniques and equipment.

We all come into skating from different backgrounds and have different objectives in our skiing. I may want to ski faster in masters races while you may want to get in a little better shape for spring. Most of us who are interested in skating want to get some aerobic benefit from our skiing. We want to do more than walk leisurely on skis, therefore we need a ski system that will help us move down the trail or across the flats at a decent clip. Whether we look for inexpensive options or jump right into the latest high performance gear, it's essential to know the basics about skating equipment. There is a confusing assortment of new products that have been stamped "skating" and placed on the market. Some are good and others leave a lot to be desired. Let's cut through some of the hype and see what we need to get up and gliding.

POLES

The skating revolution, like most revolutions, blew some things straight up into the air. Once everything settled down, ski equipment for skating had changed dramatically. Ski poles emerged as the most important piece of gear and they were longer, lighter, and stiffer.

Long ski poles allow you to skate in the correct upright position

Yes, ski poles are the most important piece of skating equipment. This comes as a surprise to most of us who never paid more than $20 for a pair of poles. We began cross country skiing with bamboo or aluminum poles which we used as much for stability, like outriggers, as for propulsion. Well, we need to change our thinking.

As we saw in the last chapter, body position is a key factor in skating. The new long ski poles allow you to get up and over your skis and, using the upper body for propulsion, apply the poling force through much of the glide.

Too often, I see folks trying to learn to skate with a pair of flimsy elbow-high poles. Not only are they hunched over like a speed skater and finding it difficult to balance, they also are getting no power whatsoever from the poles. In order to skate in the correct upright position, you need stiffer, longer ski poles whether just out for a Sunday glide on the golf course or lining up for a 50 kilometer loppet. Ski poles should be about chin high or a little higher.

"Skating ski poles should be mustache high." That's what many instructors recommend, whether you are male or female. Bert Kleerup, who runs a popular nordic mail-order business, says, "If you don't have a 'stash', we'll mail you one with the poles." There's no question that poles should be at least chin high but many question whether recreational skiers should go much longer than that. Poles, which used to be about 80% of a skier's height, are now often 88 to 92%. Try some poles about 90% of your height—that should work fine for skating—use 86% to 88% if you plan to use them for both skating and striding.

You will be surprised at how fast you adapt to long poles. Once you ski with them a few times, you'll be using them for diagonal striding as well. Remember, you can always cut down a pair of poles (the baskets and handles come off quite easily in warm water), but it's a little tricky to grow them longer. Buy a pair that's long enough.

Long poles used to be plagued by excessive flexibility. You put a lot of stress on the ski poles while skating, much more than while diagonal striding. Each time the pole bends, and believe me, it will, you waste energy. While this is critical in a long citizen race, it also can be just as important on a long tour. Most of us don't have enough upper body

Ski poles for skating should be about 90% of your height

strength as it is—we need to use what we have effectively. Other equally important factors are the weight of the poles and the ability of the grip and the basket to transfer your energy into forward motion. You'll find that stiff lightweight poles are the best investment a ski skater can make. Test them before you buy and get the stiffest that you can afford.

Fortunately, just as we need longer poles, the price and availability of skating poles is excellent. Many manufacturers have introduced skating ski poles for the entry-level market. New technology using carbon-fiber and Kevlar products has decreased the weight and strengthened the shafts, and prices have dropped. You can now buy a pair of adequate skating poles for about $50. Plan on three times that if you want the best racing poles available.

SKIS

There I was, hacksaw poised, about ready to make a real commitment to the skating revolution. It was "off with their heads" for my nearly-new pair of Jarvinens. Barely scratched and gouged from my first attempts at skating, they waited on the bench. They would never be 215 centimeters again.

Yes, I was caught up in the "voodoo" of skating. Like many skiers taking up skating, I found that I had skis too long and poles too short. I was going to do something about it. During those days, it was fashionable among some citizen racers to cut down the tips of their diagonal skis to try to improve the handling. I went one step further—after brazenly hacking off a sizeable part of the tip, I cut several centimeters off the tail as well. My long traditional skis were now nearly skating-size skis. I skated and raced on them for the rest of the season. But don't bother getting out your saw—there are better ways to equip yourself with skis for skating. Perhaps for the time being, until you are sure about skating, what you have right now is all that you need.

The new crop of skating skis is a far cry from the pine-tarred hickory beauties of a decade ago. Not only are they short and super light, many of them rival their alpine cousins for flash and glitz. Most are built for a single purpose—skating—and they are excellent for just that. With new flex patterns and longer running surfaces, they make skating even faster and more fun. Skating skis are stiffer torsionally, providing a better platform for pushing. They are like a fancy sports car—delightful for whipping around but not too practical when there's lots of snow. Skating skis are single-purpose and unsuited, due to the lack of any wax pocket, for anything but skating and double poling.

You don't need skating skis to become quite adept at skating. Thousands of skiers skate on their waxable diagonal skis and see no need to upgrade to special equipment. Any good light touring or racing ski can be used for skating, and if you're buying, some excellent bargains are available. On the other hand, others, realizing that shorter lighter skis make skating easier, will opt to purchase a pair of skating skis. For them, prices have become much more reasonable. There are also excellent buys in combination recreational skis designed to be used for both skating and classical techniques. If you buy a dual-purpose pair of skis, keep them short.

Before we go further, let's review some of the terms used when discussing skis. The more homework you do, the better decision you'll be ready to make.

Several years ago, in the early days of the skating movement, some cynics suggested that manufacturers simply stamped a "skating" logo on traditional gear and presto, had a new product. There's no question that a wave of new technology, from poles to skis to waxes, was spawned by skating. In order to make intelligent decisions, it helps to be able to speak and read, the lingo of ski construction.

Do we really care whether our skis are made with injection molding or torsion box construction? Of course not. What we need to know is what's the best ski for our athletic ability and pocketbook. It doesn't hurt to ask a few questions. When I'm looking for skis, I ask citizen racers how they like the racing skis they've got on, whether the skis are hard to handle, where they bought them, etc. Expect ski store personnel to be able to talk about side cut, camber, and flex patterns. If they look bewildered if you mention these terms, you'd better look elsewhere.

The *width* of the ski is measured in millimeters. The widest skis, touring skis, are usually 50 to 55 mm wide since they need to support your weight in untracked snow. Light touring skis, more suited for packed areas, are narrower, about 48-50 mm. Racing skis are the narrowest, often 44 mm wide.

The difference in the width of skis from tip to tail is called *sidecut*. You can easily see this by putting a pair of touring

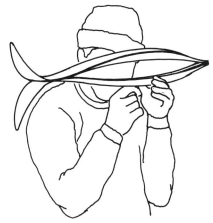

If skis do not meet exactly at the tips and tails, they may be warped

skis side by side on the floor—most likely the tips and tails will be touching but there will be a gap in the middle. That gap is the sidecut and it ranges from zero for many racing skis to 10 mm for touring skis. Sidecut makes the ski turn easier because the tip and tail dig in when the ski is on edge.

For years, *length* of skis has been measured by the "arm-in-the-air" method. Many ski stores and rental shops still have you raise your arm and recommend that the tip of the ski come to your upraised wrist. If they do, look elsewhere. This method is pretty old-fashioned for today, whether for skating or traditional equipment. On the other hand (so to speak), there is no handy formula that works—ski length depends upon not only your height but your weight, your athletic ability, and the type of snow conditions you generally ski on. A heavier skier may use a slightly longer ski than a lightweight; a better skier often will use slightly longer skis. Most men use skis that are 190 to 200 centimeters long for skating while women skate on 160 to 180 cm skis. Don't buy skis that are too long, shorter skis are easier to handle.

Camber is the arch of the ski that distributes your weight on the snow when you glide. Flexibility is what allows the ski to bend. Flexible skis are called soft-cambered skis while stiffer skis are called, just that, stiff skis. In order to get proper performance out of your skis, the camber must match your weight. In terms of importance, getting skis 5 centimeters shorter or longer is not as crucial as matching your weight to the camber of the ski so that it distributes your weight equally.

Body weight plays the most important role in choosing a skating ski because the force applied is much closer to your weight that in diagonal striding. (1.5 times body weight for skating versus 2 to 3 times for diagonal according to some studies.) You want a ski that distributes your weight over the length of the ski. Many skating skis are just too stiff in the tips and tails—they will break the snow instead of gliding over it. Racers carry several pairs of skating skis so that they can match the ski characteristics to the snow conditions—we need to find a good compromise for our normal skating conditions. The best way to select skis is to go out and ski on them. Good ski shops will help you with the decision. They may even have pairs of "loaners" of different lengths and flex patterns that you can try out before making the final selection.

What about no-wax skis? Over the years, the majority of the cross country skis sold in the U.S. have been no-wax models. Unfortunately, they are impossible for skating—don't even bother to try. Every time you put your weight on a ski to try to glide, the patterned bottom digs in, as it's designed to, and the ski stops. I took a rasp and coarse sandpaper to my son's skis to remove the fishscale bottom and convert them to skaters, but it's a lot of work. If you own no-wax skis, save them for the days when you just want to go out and tour. And start shopping for a pair of skating skis.

If you own waxable skis, your choices are a little more

difficult. First, your diagonal skis are probably about 5 to 10 centimeters longer than those you'd buy for skating. You can certainly skate on long skis, we've done it for years. However, you tend to get a lot of interference, especially on uphill sections, as the tails of the skis scrape and hit each other. If you have a fast pair of waxable skis, you might try them for skating for a while and see how you like the technique. But, if you find you're doing a lot of skating, start looking for a pair of skating skis. Make your skating skis about 5-10 centimeters shorter than diagonal skis.

It is easy to get mired in the technical aspects of ski selection. Most recreational skiers and citizen racers could care less if their skis have sidecut or whether they have soft tips or stiff torsional flex. We want skis that will be comfortable, long-lasting, and fun to ski on.

Regardless of your skiing background or what skis you have in the basement, if most of your skiing will be skating or if you plan to get into citizen racing, by all means buy some skating skis. You'll love them. They are designed for skating and they do make it a lot easier. I've skated one year on diagonal skis and one year on skating skis—there definitely is a pleasant difference.

BOOTS AND BINDINGS

In spite of what you may hear, you do not need special bindings and boots to skate on skis. Old three-pin "rat-trap" bindings and old leather boots work fine for me when there's new snow and not much of it. I go out and beat up my old touring skis on the grass and rocks—skating away with 1970's equipment.

But, as in other equipment areas, skating boots and bindings have flooded the market in recent years. A whole new generation of lower-cost skating boots has arrived. Most manufacturers sell integrated systems so not all boots fit all bindings. There are several major systems, all of which

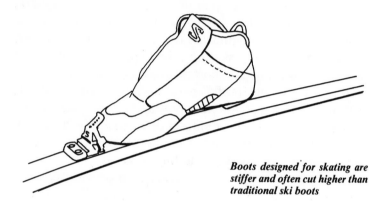

Boots designed for skating are stiffer and often cut higher than traditional ski boots

work for skating.

Boots designed for skating are often cut higher than regular boots. You don't necessarily need this level of equipment, especially if you are just starting skating. Skating boots are, like skating skis, single purpose. Because of their stiffness, they are not comfortable for diagonal striding. What you do need is a boot that is stiff enough to resist the torque of skating. Check out one of the new moderate-priced boots that can be used for both skating and striding.

The original 3-pin bindings, 75 millimeters wide, are still being supplied with many low cost ski packages. They are being supplanted by a host of new integrated binding systems such as the New Nordic Norm (NNN) and the Salomon Nordic System (SNS). The systems designed specifically for skating are stiffer and designed to handle the lateral stresses of skating. They keep the boot rigid on the ski so, like skating boots, they're not very functional for diagonal striding.

Many of the new bindings can be used for both skating and striding. In some, flex plates can be changed to vary stiffness. If you decide to go with combination skis, choose a combination diagonal/skating binding as well.

New binding systems are about equal in price, quality, and function, in spite of the advertising claims. Probably the most important factor in your selection decision is comfort— how do the boots feel on your feet? You're going to be skating many kilometers on them so choose wisely. Also consider compatibility—what do your kids ski on? Your friends? Your instructor or coach? Switching skis is a good way to find out how different ski lengths, cambers, and glide wax combinations work. You need compatible bindings for that.

Many of the new integrated binding systems are not interchangeable

THE COSTS OF SKATING EQUIPMENT

For years, cross country skiing has been promoted by the fact that it is inexpensive. For performance skiing such as skating, that's really not the case. An entry-level package will list for $250-300 (U.S.) but you should be able to buy it for less than that. If you want racing-level gear, it's not hard to double that amount.

Up until recently, there hasn't been a lot of extra skating gear available for off-season buying. Now, with the plethora of skating skis and boots available, it may pay to buy in late summer or early fall when you can often get the best price. Still, don't expect to find "bargain-basement" specials on skating equipment. There are limited quantities produced and that, plus the recent decline in the U.S. dollar, affects prices. You are paying for state-of-the-art equipment so look at it as a long term investment.

Late spring is also a good time to shop for bargains. As you will find out, some of the best skating is in the spring, when many cross country skiers, unwilling to put up with sticky klister, have put their skis away. Find a ski shop getting ready to put bikes or canoes out on the display floor, work a deal on skating gear, and you still may have a month of great skating on skis.

Before you buy, do some homework on your own—talk to skiers, dig through old copies of *Cross Country Skier,* see if there is a nordic ski club in your area and talk to some of the members. See if you can find a roller ski race in the summer and talk to the participants about shops they'd recommend.

Find a shop that knows skating. Some, especially the smaller specialty shops, have had to do their homework to stay solvent, and they pride themselves on their knowledge. Look for a place that sells to racers but can still talk to recreational skiers, a store that sells bikes, canoes, backpacking gear and has salespersons who are skiers, preferably racers. Visit them on off-peak hours and explain your situation—that you want to get into skating, you want to race, are transitioning from alpine skiing—whatever your situation is. Ask them to help you select gear to arrive at what is best for your body and your budget. The shop will mount the bindings and should prepare the bases so that you can walk out the door and be ready to ski. You may have to pay a little extra for that, but it's worth it to know that your skis have the right camber and flex pattern for you, your bindings are on to stay, and your skis are prepared properly.

If you are far from ski shops that carry ski gear, consider buying from one of the mail order firms. Their prices are fair and their equipment selection is extensive. But don't pick the brains of folks in ski shops to get good advice, and then go out and buy your selection by mail—not only is it boorish, it hurts the shops financially. Remember, you may need a place to get some quick repairs done in mid-season.

So, we've seen that there is no big deal to buying skating equipment. You can go out and skate on any pair of glide-waxed skis and they'll probably get you started fine. When you're tired of skating, you can throw on some grip wax and diagonal stride. If you decide to spring for a skating system, and you very well may once you get a taste of the speed and ease of the technique, you'll find a wide selection of moderately priced gear available. There are a number of new skating products aimed right at the recreational skier. The gear not only looks sharp, it also can, in many cases, be used for both skating and striding. If you do some reading, talk to knowledgeable skiers, you can hardly go wrong. Skating is so much easier on the right equipment. Why not find out for yourself?

4 Ski preparation

For every skier who took up skating because it's fast and fun, there's another one who loves it because it simplifies waxing. At the recreational level, skating gives us a "strap 'em on and go" option; we can go out and ski day after day on the same glide wax. No longer do we need to deal with myriad kickwaxes, we can wax our skis once and be through with it. That's one approach. On the other hand, if we are going to race or are just interested in better performance, we can spend as much time working on skis as we might when waxing for diagonal striding. But we have a choice. Many recreational skaters strike a happy medium—after learning about base preparation and waxing they then decide, based on their skiing objectives, just how fancy they want to get with waxing. Before a race, they may tinker with the bases and get them just right; if they're going out for a little skate after work, they go with whatever's on the skis. But, before shying away from waxing, recall that we have given a lot of attention to gliding on a flat ski. Gliding is easier if that ski base is in fact flat and is properly prepared.

What makes a ski glide fast? One ski designer, Karhu's Heikki Suominen, has said that construction of the ski—the camber, the flex, and the shape—accounts for 70%. According to him, another 10% of the speed comes from the base material and waxing while 20% comes from the structure of the base. So, by spending some time working on our skis, we can affect 30% of the factors that make it a fast or slow ski. That's why racers pay so much attention to ski base preparation. Whether we race or not, it's a lot easier and a lot more fun to skate on fast skis. The extra glide that you get with every stroke is money in the bank—your energy bank. Fortunately, there's very little mystique in glide waxing: it involves structuring the base, ironing on some glide wax, scraping it off when it's cool, brushing the ski bottoms, and then going out skating.

BASE STRUCTURING

The winner of the last America's Cup, *Stars and Stripes,* used a unique plastic covering on the hull. The plastic film was scored by small V-shaped grooves called "riblets" which, by reducing skin friction drag, added as much as .2 knots to the yacht's speed. Ski skaters reduce drag in a similar way by adding structure (grooves) to the plastic ski base. It's not too high tech, all it takes is sandpaper and elbow grease.

Skating skis have bases made of polyethylene or similar material, commonly called P-Tex. These surfaces, whether light colored or black, look smooth to the eye but actually have thousands of microscopic pores—some technicians compare them with a sponge. If you hold skis up to a light and sight down the base, you'll see that the bases come from the factory with slight ripples or imperfections caused by the machine-grinding process. Usually the groove has also been marked by the mechanical router. So the first task, and it's a one-time job, is to get the skis as smooth and flat as possible, to get rid of any high spots or low spots on the ski bottoms.

You'll need a place to work on your skis, preferably waist-high or so. Ski stands are available but most skiers use a workbench, saw horses, or some wooden planks on edge.

Skating skis are quite flexible so it helps to have them supported as much as possible when you start sanding and scraping. If you do not use a special stand, have a tailboard at the end of the bench so that you can scrape the skis against a retainer. If you try to use a common vise, remember that the sidewalls of skis are very fragile.

First, clean any dust or grime off the bases with a liquid wax remover. Then, use 100 grit silicon carbide paper and a sanding block to sand the base smooth, using long, easy strokes from tip to tail. (If possible, don't use regular sandpaper because it leaves too much grit on the ski.) Hold the base up to the light to check for imperfections; high spots will show lighter in color. Some skiers draw a sharp flat

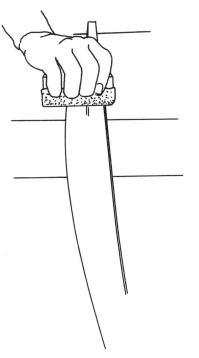

Sand the base using long easy strokes from tip to tail

metal scraper from tip to tail to remove any burrs and highlight any remaining irregularities. You'll find that you need to change sandpaper rather frequently as it gets clogged with P-Tex. Spend some time sanding the groove as well, using a pencil wrapped in sandpaper for rounded grooves. Sand and sand until you're satisfied that you've got the bases nice and flat.

Next, take off any burrs with a fiber pad such as Scotchbrite or Fibertex, and then clean off the grit with wax remover. (Look at the skis you just sanded and you'll see that they are already structured from the sandpaper.) If you want to get skiing, you can wax the skis right now and be ready to go. If you want to get more involved in base preparation, read on.

Base structuring is the term used to describe the process of putting grooves into the skis to match the snow conditions. In theory, the width of the grooves should be slightly smaller than the size of the snow crystals. However, unless you are going on the World Cup circuit, just use the recommendations that follow, you'll be close enough.

Glass-smooth bases are never as fast as those with some texture, some grooves. The warmer and wetter the snow, the more crucial this is. Visualize a couple of panes of glass placed together with a film of water between them. Suction makes them very difficult to pull apart. The same goes for skis, which ride on a thin film of water. Grooves, like those on **Stars and Stripes**, break up the suction between the skis and the free water in the snow during above freezing conditions. We put this texture, called rilling, on the skis in a variety of ways. I have a friend who uses what he calls "natural rilling", the scratches and scrapes that his skis pick up in normal skiing, for most conditions. Only when it's wet does he get more sophisticated.

Base structuring is done by sanding or by rilling to match snow conditions. Fine grooves are put in for cold conditions while wider rills are used for warmer skiing. Let's consider colder snow conditions first. For normal conditions just below freezing you'll want a fine structure on the base which can be obtained by sanding with a #150 sandpaper. Draw the carbide paper from tip to tail. For colder temperatures, a finer sandpaper such as a #220 is used, while for frigid conditions, use #320. Clean off the grit with wax remover or hot wax and you're ready for final waxing.

Wet conditions call for more attention to structuring due to the free moisture in the snow. The easiest way is just to use the rilling from the #100 sandpaper. Another way is to use the edge of a flat file to cut small grooves into the base, pulling the file from tip to tail. This takes a bit of practice to keep the rills going straight down the ski and the depths of the grooves even. A better way is to use a riller. This specially-designed tool cuts a series of fine grooves, rills, into the base of the ski. You just draw it along the ski from tip to tail, pressing firmly, and you'll have a uniform pattern cut into the ski. There are rill sizes for various snow temperatures but a standard riller works well for nearly all conditions. Rillers are quite expensive for the number of times you'll need them; you should be able to use one at the shop where you bought your skis and where you buy glide wax. The last step, whether you sand, file, or use a riller, is to remove the fine hairs and fibers that the structuring raises from the base. Whisk these whiskers away with a fiber pad and you're ready to wax.

Many racers clean their ski bases by hot wax instead of wax remover. Polyethylene bases are porous and pick up a lot of grime from the snow. This is particularly noticeable on light bases. To clean them before final waxing, iron on a soft skating wax and keep it molten on the ski for a moment. Then, while the wax is still hot and liquid, wipe the ski base with Fiberlene. (Careful, it's hot.) Now you are ready to glide wax.

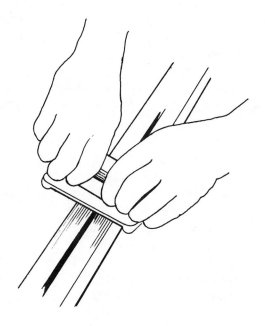

A riller cuts a uniform pattern of grooves in to the ski base

GLIDE WAXING

Glide waxing can be quite simple. You can iron on the universal glider, scrape it off, and go out skiing. Or, like base structuring, the process can be much more detailed, matching wax characteristics with the snow. If you plan to race, you'll find that glide wax does make a big difference in the speed of skis, and you'll spend time matching snow temperature with wax, just as with grip wax.

Cross country racers used alpine wax for gliding when skating first became popular. But alpine wax is designed for short fast bursts down the mountain and won't hold up for the longer nordic race distances. In the last few years, a whole new generation of glide wax has been designed to handle the slower speeds and higher pressures of skating. At first there were only a few colors of glide wax, but now there's a rainbow of colors coded to match snow temperatures and conditions. To get even more specific, you can mix different color waxes to come closer to the snow temperature. Each manufacturer has a separate system and some brands are faster than others—check with your racing friends for tips. Watch for new products such as graphite flecks, all aimed at making gliding easier. There will be a lot of new wax products for skating in the next few years.

There are several schools of thought on waxing. Most waxing clinics are given by ski wax sales people, and they put lots of wax on, scrape it off, and do it again. (Which tends to use a lot of wax at $5.00 a color) Other skiers are more frugal, warming the wax slightly and crayoning it on, before heating it on the ski. But, when you consider the price of ski equipment, wax is pretty cheap—don't be afraid to use a little extra. Use enough to get a good coating on the ski base—you don't want that iron in direct contact with the P-Tex base.

A waxing iron is a necessity for skating ski preparation. You can buy an iron at a ski shop or use any K-Mart Special that has a reliable temperature control. Don't, even if you see skiers do it, use a waxing torch directly on the ski base unless you have a P-Tex death wish. Likewise, waxing irons that are heated with a propane torch are fine when you are waxing outside in a ski area parking lot but tend to be difficult to keep at a constant temperature. Whatever you use, be careful, you can damage the skis with too much heat. There's nothing more sickening than to see an expensive ski base pop up (that's the voice of experience) where you have just overheated it. In addition to delaminating the base, you can also seal the surface pores with too much heat. Use a temperature (about 250 degrees) that will melt the wax easily but will not make it smoke. The trick is to heat up the base material so that it puffs up, microscopically-speaking, and absorbs wax. You want to drive the wax deep into the pores. That will be the wax you'll ski on.

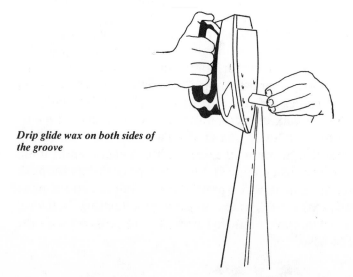

Drip glide wax on both sides of the groove

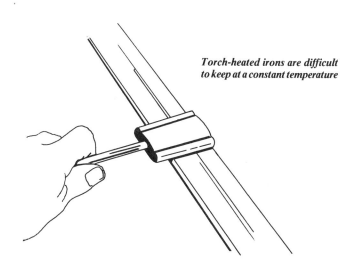

Torch-heated irons are difficult to keep at a constant temperature

Using an iron, drip glide wax on both sides of the groove and run the iron back and forth on a molten layer of wax. You'll find that wax for warmer conditions is easier to use—it seems to be drawn into the pores easily. On the other hand, cold wax just lies there and drips off the edge of the ski on to the workbench. Work one section of the ski at a time, adding wax as needed to keep a liquid layer on the ski. Keep an eye on the heat and take your time—you'll get a feel for it before long. Check under the tip or tail of the ski, they should be quite warm to the touch but not hot. Take your time before you move on—the wax should be on the ski for several minutes in a molten state. When you have finished, set the ski aside and work on the other.

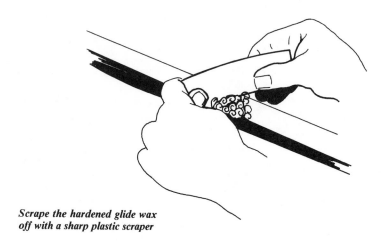

Scrape the hardened glide wax
off with a sharp plastic scraper

Try to scrape the wax out of the groove while it is still warm since once it hardens, it is difficult to remove without having the scraper slip and mark up the base. You can use the end of a P-Tex candle to take wax out of round grooves while the point of a plastic scraper works for V-grooves. This is also a good time, while the wax is warm, to gently scrape drippings off the sidewalls. Most coaches let the ski cool for about 20 to 30 minutes before scraping the glide wax off. Other skiers wipe the wax off while it is soft and do the final scraping later. In either case, after the wax is cooled, scrape off all the wax except for a fine film. Again, glide wax for warm snows, being softer, is easier to scrape off than colder waxes.

Glide wax is scraped from the base with a sharp, flat plastic scraper, working from tip to tail. The wax will peel off in shavings and, since it is electrically charged, it will stick to everything in sight. (This is why skiers who secretly wax in motel rooms wipe off the wax before it hardens.) Go over the skis with the scraper a number of times to remove all visible wax from the surface of the base. You want to be skiing on the wax in the pores of the ski. Take it easy, too much pressure on the scraper will remove the base structure you just put on.

Wax has coated the base structure so the final job in ski preparation is to brush your skis to open up that structured base by removing the wax from the grooves. The colder the snow, the finer the brush you want. You will be surprised at how much wax you raise—it will look like dandruff on the ski. Brush them clean, wipe gently with Fiberlene, and you are ready to go.

Since the side of the skating ski is on edge during the push phase, racers also wax the sidewalls of their skis with either glide wax or a paste wax. If you are looking for that last iota of glide, do it.

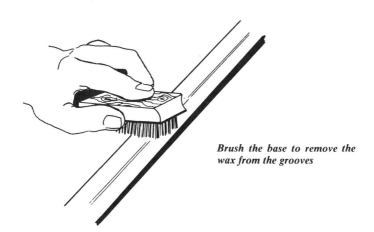

Brush the base to remove the wax from the grooves

WAX KITS

When skating first began to become popular, skiers felt that they could get away from the large collections of wax and equipment that went with diagonal skiing. If you've read this far, you can see that for performance skating, that's not necessarily the case. In fact, you'll need a case, or box, to hold your glide waxing equipment. Let's look at what is needed:

Waxing Bench or Vise
Liquid Wax Remover
Lint-free wiping material (SWIX Fiberlene for example)
Waxing Iron
Scraper—plastic
Scraper—metal (if you are careful with it)
Scotch-Brite or Fibertex pad
Silicon Carbide Sandpaper (#100, 150, 220)
Sandpaper block (can be used with Fibertex as well)
Nylon brush
Brass brush
Glide waxes
Flat file (for rilling and sharpening scraper)

If you step right out and buy a complete glide wax kit from a ski shop, it will cost over $100. On the other hand, you probably have some of the material from prior skiing or around the house. Look for non-ski places to buy much of it, hardware store sandpaper works just as well as ski shop paper. I bought my waxing iron, which I use on $200 skis, for $1.50 at a Salvation Army outlet. I sometimes save money on wax by going halves with a friend, we buy two colors and simply split them up between us. Don't be afraid to borrow irons and rillers—build up your waxing supplies over a period of time.

The name of the game in skating is glide. We can improve glide with better technique and we can stretch glide by attending to our ski bases. Well-prepared skis are fun to ski on.

They track better because of the grooves, and they climb better because they are faster. Some experts estimate that we only glide about 20% of the time in skating, the rest of the time we are pushing (and gliding). They say that your skis should feel fast while pushing. It is a great feeling to switch skis with some friends and find that yours are the quickest of the bunch. You can't wait to get them back on again. That 30% speed factor that we can alter by waxing and base structuring can provide big paybacks in speed and self-satisfaction. And for most of us, conditions don't change that drastically from outing to outing. Prepare and wax your skis well and they will be good for days of fast skating. If the tracks are harsh and icy, the wax will wear faster. You will notice a faint whiteness or streaks on the inner edges of the base where you skate—that will tell you that it is time to get out the iron again.

We have seen that glide waxing is easy to learn and has to be done only a few times a season for non-racers. Ski preparation gives you a chance to check over your skis, to "personalize them" for your use. For many skiers, this tinkering with ski bases is an integral part of the preparation for skiing, ranking right behind training. They will wax new skis a dozen times before the season starts, just to break them in and get a well-saturated base to race on. Top racers are spending more time than ever working on their skis, trying, as the **Stars and Stripes** designers did, to grab every fraction of drag reduction that they can. From recreational skaters to World Cuppers, fast skis are fun skis to skate on.

5 When and where to skate

Armed with some skating equipment and the techniques covered in the previous chapters, you should be ready to skate. So why do we need a chapter on when and where to skate? Isn't that pretty obvious? Well, once the snow comes, there are countless places to cross country ski—the local golf course, city parks, county trail systems, the nearest touring center. You can go out and diagonal stride whether there's two inches or two feet. But it's not always that easy with skating. Skaters not only need snow, we need packed snow. Just like you can't take a light racing bike out on the back dirt roads of Vermont, there are many places that you can't take your skating skis. On the other hand, in certain conditions, skating opens up whole vistas of skiing—frozen lakes, crusty woods, and snowmobile trails allow you to skate unimpeded for miles and miles.

I do a lot of skiing in an area of upstate New York called the Tug Hill plateau which is famous for its snowfall (most snow east of the Rockies) and its hundreds of kilometers of trails and woods roads. Early last winter, I was raring to go skating. Having trained all fall by running and roller skiing, I was ready to work on some of the skating techniques that I had learned the year before. We had no snow on the ground at home near Syracuse, but there was over a foot of new snow when I arrived that Saturday morning in December. Some Friday night snowmobilers had made a nice trail in from the parking area, and I V-skated in on my cut-off diagonal skis. They were glide-waxed and working fine. Things were great for the first kilometer when I realized that the snow machines had called it quits and turned back—all there was ahead was a single set of ski tracks.

Bound to practice my skating, I tried to marathon skate in the soft snow but it was impossible. Then I tried double poling but that also got old pretty fast as my ski poles sank deeply into the new snow. It was time to jump off the skating bandwagon. Luckily, I had a tin of kick wax with me so, after pausing to rub a layer on, I had a nice afternoon of diagonal striding. It was a good lesson—first, to carry some wax when you're planning to skate off the beaten path and secondly, don't give up on traditional techniques, they may be what gets you home in certain conditions.

On the other hand, late the next spring, deep in the heart of mud season, I went for a workout up north in conditions that could only be called slushy. It was like skiing on a grey sno-cone, but it was snow.

A couple of college coaches were out for a training run with their traditional skis. As they wrestled with tubes of red klister, I just strapped on my skating skis, which I hadn't waxed or rilled for several weeks, and went off skiing. They came back with half the forest floor on their skis. One mumbled as he tried to clean things up before stowing his skis, "Now I remember another reason why I like skating." I just slid my skis in the ski bag and was done with it. Yes, not only is skating great in the spring, it also is hassle-free.

However, there are some conditions that make skating a chore. Let's review a few of those so you can deal with them.

POOR CONDITIONS FOR SKATING

Freshly Packed Dry Snow

While it is impossible to skate in deep fresh snow, it is nearly as tough when the new dry snow has just been packed. If you ski at family-type touring centers, most of which pack their trails with snowmobiles, you are bound to encounter beautiful fresh snow that is "mushy." Your skis cut into the soft surface and your poles sink out of sight. (There are some snowless winters where we'd love to have such a problem.) Skating on this deep snow that has not firmed up can be frustrating, especially if you're new to ski skating.

Experienced skiers handled soft snow by keeping their skating "quick and light," using their poles gingerly. They use their upper body less and their legs more for propulsion, just as if they were skiing without poles. If there are tracks set, get into them and try a marathon skate, again being

In soft new snow, ski as if you were without poles — use your legs for propulsion

careful with the poling. The soft snow makes double poling virtually impossible—the small baskets on your ski poles leave you with nothing to push against.

Learn to ski in soft new snow because you'll undoubtedly run into it. Quicken the tempo because your glide will be slow in these conditions. Use the diagonal skate to keep things light and easy, and work on keeping a flat ski. Then, if the temperature drops that evening to harden the packed snow, come back the next day for some great skating. You will have earned it.

Below Zero

When the temperature hovers around zero, skating is a chore. Regardless of how you glide wax, it is difficult to get any glide. You have to power along with a lot of double poling. Usually, if the sun is out, you hit sheltered spots where the snow has warmed slightly, tantalizing you with some nice skating conditions, and then you're back in the shade and laboring again. You wonder why you are trying to skate when you come to hills and can walk right up them without grip wax.

This might be a good time to put on some kick wax and practice your diagonal stride, even if you have skating skis. If you want to skate, work on getting the most out of your poling, really collapsing over the ski poles to get some thrust. Use the diagonal skate more than normal since skating on the level is similar to climbing a hill on other days. But any way you do it, skating on super cold snow is usually nothing but hard work.

Wet Fresh Snow

To finish our review of the days that skating is a drag, pun intended, we'll look at freshly fallen wet snow. There can be a couple of problems with these conditions, even if the snow is well groomed. The snow can be quite slow due to the high water content. You have to structure your ski bases (See previous chapter) to cut down on the suction. The packed snow is also often "squirrely" causing balance problems. It seems like a constant effort to skate on a flat ski and your ankles get quite tired. Even so, in spite of less than ideal conditions, it still beats messing around with klister. Check out the tracks, they may be glazed and fast on days like this.

GOOD CONDITIONS FOR SKATING

While we've looked at some of the difficult conditions for skating, it's important to note than in a typical winter, most days have conditions that are good for skating. These are the same days, I call them "blue sky, green wax" days, where diagonal stride skiing is good as well. There are some days when skating is great—many of these occur in the spring.

Spring Skating

The cardinals are out and about and the robins have returned. It's mud season, maple sugaring season, time to put the skis away for another year. Not quite so fast. This is the season for skating even if you have to drive a ways to find snow. Spring provides the best skating of the year. Your balance is honed from a season's practice, and the granular snow is fast.

Cold nights and sunny days make the sap run and they also make skating skis run. There's no need to worry about glide wax, just ski on what's on the skis. You will love the freedom of stepping into your bindings and just skating through the woods. Spring snow, when it's settled and hard, allows you to skate virtually anywhere. Keep an eye open for icy patches that haven't loosened up or soft corn snow on the sheltered sunny areas.

It is a good time to stop and enjoy the sun. Unlike the deep winter when the woods are quite still, now there's a lot going on. Crows are moving about, phoebes call to one another from the hardwoods, and chipmunks and squirrels are foraging. These are also good conditions for working on technique. Spring snow is easy to skate on and you can really work on extending your glide. The sun is up higher and lets you critique your form by watching your shadow. For many of us who hated to mess with klister, it is a whole new season.

Spring is a great season for skating on skis

But it's short. In many parts of ski country there are usually only a couple of weeks of good spring cross country skiing. Take advantage of it—go out in the morning when the hard snow is being warmed but watch out later in the day. That great crust that allowed you to whip through the maples, dodging saplings, skating up a storm, can turn soft under the warm spring sun, and your skis will cut right into it. I usually carry a tin of red wax just in case I'm far from the car and decide I need to trudge back home.

WHERE TO SKATE

Skating opens up a whole network of snowmobile trails and miles of woods roads for you. Skating works much better than striding on these machine packed trails; as long as you have a track a couple of snow machines wide, you're in business. As you know if you've tried these trails, snowmobiles churn up a lot of debris and usually the snow is gritty and tough on the skis. And remember, the snow-mobiles tend to run fast so keep your eyes open as you share their space.

On the other hand, while many new places to skate are added, you are excluded from many cross country ski trails, especially the narrow winding county and state park trails that are tracked by skiers but unpacked. For many skiers, these challenging routes are the best part of nordic skiing, but you can't skate them because they are just too narrow. You need to look for wider trails that are interesting—packed courses that provide some climbs and descents.

More and more touring centers, after some initial concern, are welcoming skating. They often pack one side of the trail for skating and on the other, set tracks for diagonal stride. Others simply designate certain trails for skating. Skating does require wider courses, especially on the uphills, and some areas simply are not set up, without doing a lot of clearing, to handle both skating and traditional. However, by respecting other skiers and keeping off preset tracks, we can do a lot to keep trails open for glide-waxed skis.

Whether you try skating for general touring and recreation or are a hard-charging citizen racer, you'll run into situations where the long graceful glides of skating get you tangled up with other skiers. It usually occurs when trying to pass—suddenly long poles and short skis are intertwined, and both skiers are tottering. Or, it can happen with your own equipment—like at the finish of the 1987 Whoppers American Birkebeiner where Pal Sjulstad, in a three-way sprint to the finish, tripped on his own ski pole and fell just before crossing the line.

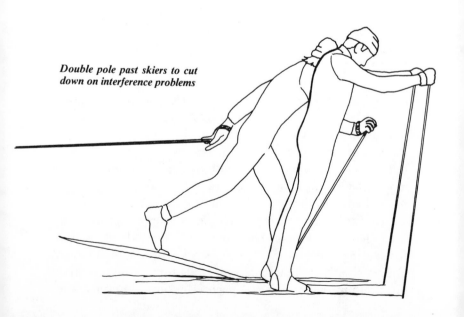

Double pole past skiers to cut down on interference problems

If elite skiers can get tangled up, it's even easier for the rest of us. It can happen like this. You skate up behind a skier who is striding along, minding his or her own business, and you are faced with a choice. You can double pole past if it is level or downhill and avoid problems altogether. You can skate by, being careful, especially on narrower trails, to keep your skis out of the woods on one side, and off the person's skis on the other side. You'll find that at many touring centers, people will step off to the side of the trail to let you pass (making you feel like a road hog). A few will resent your use of the whole trail, especially if you are cutting up their track. Use the marathon skate and double pole and stay off their turf.

When you first learn to skate, it seems like technique goes out the window when you are faced with a possible conflict with another skier. This is usually the time that you plant your pole inside your ski and suddenly, you're putting on a show. Keep your speed up when passing either a strider or a skater—then you can double pole as you pass or at least narrow your skate until you get by. And smile and say "Hi."

There are many other places to skate. Alpine ski areas can be a good place to practice technique. Get permission from the operator and practice skating up the bunny hill. I practice on a nearby school field, going round and round the perimeter at workout speed. I can arrive home from work, jog down with my ski gear and, without fiddling with wax, get an hour of skating in. It's a good aerobic workout, something I could never easily get with diagonal stride. Without a lot of fuss, you can just go out and skate—look for places that will work for you.

6 Improving your skating

Bill Gairdner, president of the World Masters Cross Country Ski Association, once responded to a pre-race question about the types of skating to be allowed by saying, "We don't care how you come down the trail. You can do backflips if that's your thing. The first one across the finish line wins."

So, while backflips may be in vogue in freestyle skiing, in "free technique," as skating is sometimes called, there are some more restrained techniques—variations on the generic double pole V-skate. More are being developed as coaches and racers experiment with technique, but they will most likely just be refinements—at the elite skier level, there have been only a few recent changes in skating technique. Things have settled down.

This chapter is for those who are interested in racing or who just plain want to go faster on their skis. We will look at ways to skate more effectively, how to coach ourselves, and will consider some technique variations that you can add to your skating repertoire. But as we start, remember, to be a good skater, you must be able to let the ski glide. Not only do you need good balance, you need to be able to relax and be smooth. As we wade through terminology like "strong side" and "weak side", keep those basics in mind. Weight transfer and balance on a gliding ski. Sound familiar yet?

V-2 POLING WITH EVERY SKATE (ONE-SKATE)

Racers use the "one-skate," poling with both poles on each skating thrust, on flat sections and on gradual uphills; expert skiers use it on all but the steepest hills. This technique is the fastest way to skate on cross country skis. Since it balances the skating action from side to side, it demands proper weight shift from ski to ski. Because of this, some coaches feel that it should be the first skating technique taught.

V-2 is not easy. It requires good balance because to do it right, you spend more time on each glide. The double poling is sharp and the recovery quick—there is not a lot of time for a complete follow-through. There is no recovery glide like on the weak side of V-1, you have to be ready to pole again. You'll use the arms more than in traditional double poling— there is not time to fully use the trunk muscles. V-2 is a technique that is tiring for most recreational skiers and few will use it for long periods, but it is an excellent way to work on balance and speed.

To give it a try, begin on a gentle downhill and with hands forward, poles angled back, push off with the poles. Keep your elbows high and bent and use your shoulder and chest muscles. You should feel that you are pulling yourself on to your gliding ski. Get the weight out on the skating ski, just as in any skating maneuver, and then recover and push off on to the other ski. Things happen fast don't they? There's really no time to push on the poles in the follow-through after the hands pass by the body as we do in regular double poling. Also, it is hard to keep the glide going long enough because we can't balance very well on one ski, so we tend to cut off the glide and pole in the other direction. See how easy it is to get huffing and puffing with this technique? That's why most recreational skiers find it pretty demanding to use for any distance.

Use a shorter double pole motion with a quick arm

Elite racers use V-2 on much of the race course

recovery. Because you're moving faster, your elbows will be higher when you reach ahead to pole than they will be when you climb hills. The poling motion is sharp with the arms and abdominal muscles used, as in a quick double poling sequence. There is not time to bend out over the poles like in normal double poling. Your leg push and arm push should finish at the same time. As you follow through, your hands should pass the legs about mid-thigh. Quickly recover your arms and get ready for the next double pole stroke.

Let's review V-2. You want to push off the edged ski and double pole simultaneously, finishing both at the same time. Use a sharp, abbreviated poling motion and quickly recover your arms for another pole push. If you find you can't keep up with the poling pace, skip a poling motion by just skating on one side now and then and pick up the V-2 again when you are ready. Keep relaxed and glide on a flat ski. The better skier you become, the more you'll use the 1-skate.

Here are a couple of drills to try. First, get in a set of tracks and work on your poling technique by practicing quick double poles. Instead of a complete poling motion with a follow-through, double pole with the arms and shoulders, quickly as in V-2. Recover fast and do it again. A second drill is to skate, on a wide packed surface, with two double poles on each side. Try to glide from one side of the trail to the other. This is tough, especially on rough surfaces, but it's a great way to work on balance.

When you watch world-class skiers race, you'll see a lot of V-2 skating. If you're out on the course and it's cold, you can hear them coming by the "swish" of the poles. The skiers swoop like swallows as they reach up and out with their poles, follow through with their hands low, and glide. As with most sports, the best athletes make it look effortless—they aren't straining or pushing hard, just waltzing down the trail. The glide is long and relaxed and the poling, while very quick, seems effortless. That's our goal.

MARATHON SKATE

Some instructors teach marathon skating as the initial skating maneuver, others leave it until later. Marathon skating is used when skiing in prepared tracks. One ski glides in the track while the other is used, in a skating motion, to provide the propulsion. It is nearly identical to the double pole V-skate except that the in-track ski (weak side) contributes no thrust but rather, just glides. The technique works well when the course is too narrow to V-skate or when you don't want to cut up pre-set tracks by skating across them.

Marathon skating has been a good way for many recreational skiers to try skating. Even with grip-waxed skis, it can be fun to angle out a ski and glide on it. And that's all there is to it—you skate on a flat ski just as in V-skating and as you skate further from the track, you roll up on the inside edge of the skating ski and push outward. Then you make a definite weight shift back to the ski in the track. Be sure to

Make a definite weight shift to the ski in the track

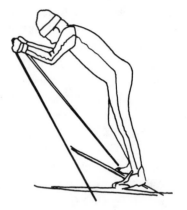

Double poling is an essential part of the marathon skate

step out with the skating foot, don't just push with an angled ski like you're riding a scooter. Just as in V-skating, the key to marathon skating is to use a powerful double pole technique. Get out over the poles and let the body weight provide part of the momentum.

Marathon skating has been labeled an obsolete technique by some yet it is still popular and useful. Watch any long World Cup or Olympic race and you'll see racers marathon skating part of the course. "It can be especially effective in cold weather," explains Kevin Jones of Cross Country Canada. "The ski in the track warms slightly and glides better."

Let's give it a try. Practice in a level area with a prepared set of tracks and get a good glide going by double poling. Plan to skate off the right ski and leave the left ski in the track. As you are gliding down the track, lift the right ski up slightly, angling the tip outward about 45 degrees. (Your feet should still be close together and the tails of the skis will probably be crossed.) Put the angled ski on the snow as you double pole in that direction. The angle will remain about 45 degrees throughout the glide phase. Transfer your weight to the angled right ski and balance. Don't be shy about committing to the skating ski— remember the "toe-knee-nose" alignment. (Some instructors recommend that you lift the "in-track" ski slightly to make sure your weight is transferred.) As the glide ends, push off with the inner edge of the right ski, just as in V-skating, and shift your weight back to the left ski which should be gliding down the track. Balance on the tracking ski, bringing your right foot all the way back in to the tracking foot, then double pole on to your right ski and try it again.

Make sure that your skating ski stays even with the ski in the track—don't let it lag behind. Step out on to it just like in any skating maneuver. The faster you travel, the further ahead the angled ski should be placed and the less angle it will have. The sequence for marathon skating goes like this: Double pole, glide on skating ski, push off, glide on "in-track" ski, double pole.

If you approach the marathon skate as just a variation of the generic V-skate, it is easy to master. It will let you skate on many narrow trails where tracks are set and since it requires less energy than some of the V-skate methods, the technique, as its name suggests, is great for longer distances. For marathon skiing, skiers usually skate on one side for a half dozen strides, then double pole a few times in the track, and then switch to skating on the other side. Marathon skating is a nice change of pace after V-skating, a chance to get into a set of tracks for a while. The muscles used are just different enough to provide a welcome relief. This is a technique that can come in handy during long tours and loppets.

STAGGERED DOUBLE POLE (OFFSET)

Hills separate good skaters from poor ones. Elite skiers float up most hills while the rest of us tend to get bogged down, resorting to a herringbone to climb. But if we add some power to our technique, we can learn to skate up most hills. It still takes, in the parlance of racers, "a good motor," so if you're not in good aerobic shape, don't expect to skate many uphills. Use the diagonal skate as long as you can, then herringbone. With proper technique, climbing is easier than you might think.

Most skaters climb hills with the double pole V-skate, called V-1 in the U.S. and called offset in Canada. It simply takes the generic V-skate and, by varying timing and body position, adds power. It also is the technique that fits when we are tired, when the snow is slow, or any time we need a little extra force in our skating. That's why it is the "bread and butter" skate of the recreational skater. Here's how it goes.

Offset is simply double-poling every other skate, V-1, with a stagger to the pole plant. It's a natural action, there is no contrived stagger in the timing of the pole plant. As before, the side we glide on while poling is called, for lack of a better term, the strong side, while the non-poling side is the weak side. Offset poling is no more complicated than straight double-poling, it just alters the double pole technique to fit the way we climb hills. I found that out the hard way. After several practice sessions with some new skis, I noticed that the tail of one looked like a woodpecker had attacked it— there were a series of round marks in the enamel. I was not reaching far enough up the hill with my lead pole and simply was planting the tip smartly on $100 worth of skating ski. I probably couldn't hear the strike on the fiberglass over my panting and wheezing.

Let's practice climbing a hill and see how it goes. We will climb with the strong side on our left. As you push off with the right ski, plant the left pole vertically, perpendicular to the ground, with your left arm bent about 90 degrees, forearm parallel to the ski pole and upper arm level with the ground. Some instructors call this "hanging on your pole." Remember the pole placement from Chapter 2? As you pole with the strong side left pole with your arm bent, plant the ski pole 5 to 10 inches ahead of your left foot, close to the body where you can develop some force. (Also to save that other ski!) Your pole and skating ski should touch the snow about together.

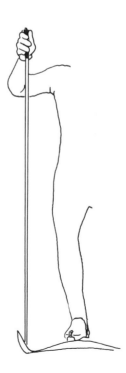

When climbing, the strong side pole is planted vertical with the forearm parallel to the ski pole

Your weak side pole (right one) is planted near your right foot, at a more acute angle in order to keep the pole tip outside the right ski. It is a very natural placement, like the position in normal double poling. As the hill steepens, the poles should be planted at the same time as the strong side ski hits the snow. Don't try to get too much out of the weak pole. You should be looking up the left ski and the poling force will be directed in line with that ski, not up the track. As you finish poling, rotate your trunk in the other direction and push off with the left ski.

The poling motion of skating is much like that of paddling

This twisting of the torso is an important element of uphill skating. Lee Borowski, ski coach and author, describes it like this in an *American Ski Coach* article. "As you plant the poles, all of your upper body weight should be applied to the pole straps. The torso then rocks forward and twists slightly. This is sometimes called the canoe paddler's twist, since it resembles the stroke used by competitive canoeists."

On shallower hills, you should strive to balance your skating, even though you are only poling on one side. Think "quick and light" and step up the hill as you push off on your other leg. As the hill steepens, the more you need out of your weak side leg. At the minimum, use the ankle for a push off, you'll be surprised at the amount of quick power it can give. In such conditions, offset skating often boils down to a momentary transfer of weight to the weak side, and then getting up and over the poles on the strong side. Good skiers bounce back and forth, quickly transferring weight, as they climb. It's almost a hop-skate. In spite of the tempo and lightness, they are still doing the basics, turning their bodies in the direction they're skating and bringing their new glide foot in to the ankle of the other leg.

Most of us favor one side or the other in V-skating. Learn to climb using both sides, otherwise you'll get very tired climbing long hills. Many skiers start the climb poling on the least favorite side and then switch as the going gets tough. Practice switching using an extra poling to get to the other side. Racers often switch sides every half dozen strokes or so just to balance the workload and conserve strength.

It is important to think in terms of natural progression in skating transitions. You don't just come to a hill and say to yourself, "Time for offset," you use the stroke that fits the situation. Don't wait for a terrain change to switch skating techniques—do it when you need to. This will come with experience.

Cross country skiing is a thinking sport, that's what makes it attractive to many. Skiers are confronted with a variety of terrain and must vary their techniques to compensate. For example, just as a runner approaching a hill shifts gears as the climb begins, shortening the stride and bending the body more, so does a skater. When you approach a hill, you may want to continue to use the stroke you use on the flat and keep your body lower, not coming up for a full upright recovery, and shortening the double pole motion. If you are tired or the hill is steep, don't be too proud to use the diagonal skate. I've been passed by skiers, late in a race, who, by keeping their diagonal skate going, have the energy left to tackle that last hill. Offset is faster because it uses the upper body so try to switch back to it as you near the top of the hill. As you transition on the crest, shift back into higher gear, skating more upright with more follow-through and longer skates.

To summarize, the term offset comes from the offsetting action of the arms as we skate up hills. The poles are planted at the same time the ski is weighted and the strong side pole is planted further up the hill. Don't think too much about this, it's very natural. Skiers do not follow-through as much and don't come as upright as on the flats. As we slow in the climb, the offset is more pronounced and then, as we speed up after the hill, we transition back to a regular V-1 skate.

SKATING DOWNHILL

When racing, citizen racers welcome the chance to get into a track and glide downhill in a tuck position—it's a nice chance to catch your breath and let your skating muscles relax. In shallower descents, they also double pole down the track. Now, with skating, we have several other alternatives for the slight downhills and the flats.

A common way to handle slight downgrades is to skate them without poles, just as we did when learning. Like V-2, skating without poles requires very good balance so you may want to wait until you have some experience skating before tackling it. Skiers use different techniques—some hold their poles away from the body by the handles and let the poles swing with the arms. Others prefer to tuck their poles under their arms and skate in a slight tuck. In either case, rotate your body in the direction you are skating and let your arms swing naturally. Skating without poles

When skating downhill, let your poles swing naturally

provides a nice rest for the arms and allows you to keep your speed going without a lot of effort. For new skaters, it is also a good way to build confidence in your balance. "Hey, I don't need those poles to stay upright."

Another variation of the double pole V-skate is also used to skate downhills where you are going too fast to pole every skate (V-2). This technique is called the 2-skate in Canada and is sometimes also referred to as the "open field skate." You double pole on just one side, delaying the pole plant slightly. Because of your speed, instead of poling on to the gliding ski, skate off on the ski and plant the pole part way through the glide. You'll have a long glide which will require good balance. The key is not to rush. Place the glide ski on the snow and then double pole, using a complete poling movement. Pause, gliding, before recovering the poles forward. Toni Scheier, a top Canadian coach, suggests that you imagine that you are underwater, so that your arm recovery will be slowed and so you won't rush.

LOOKING GOOD

Let's consider form for a minute. We would all like to look like ace skiers Gunde Svan or Anette Boe as we skate down the trail. Ah, the tricks that nature plays—we may look more like the Hunchback of Notre Dame slumped over our poles. Each of us has our own set of physical gifts and luggage to cart along.

Have you ever been running along and been passed by a person who looks awkward? Perhaps an arm flops out like Bill Rogers or a foot drags a bit. Then you think, "She may look strange but she's ahead of me." The same thing can happen in any activity: the guy with the weird tennis serve that aces you, the woman with the funny golf swing that out-drives everyone. So what's the point?

We need to ski our own way, to find out what works for us and go with it. V-2 may never fit our way of skiing and be too much work to be fun. There's a lot of freedom in skating—by its very free-form nature, it encourages individualistic styles. While it helps to see skating done by the best in the world, don't try to be a Pierre Harvey clone. Get an idea of how you should look to go fast and then, do your own thing.

There are lots of ways to work on your skating. You first need to develop a picture of how you want to look as you skate. This can be done by visiting races, watching videos, getting someone to take a look at you. Perhaps the best is to get yourself videotaped.

A picture is worth a thousand words—especially if it is a picture of you. "I'm sold on video-taping," says instructor Bob Rude, "especially for skating since it's so balance-oriented. You take a head-on shot, a tail-on shot, and then a side view and boy, it's like standing naked beside the Interstate. All your good and bad points are there for the world to see." More and more skiers are using home video equipment to critique their skiing or frequenting ski schools which use the technique. There are a number of good videos available commercially showing the various skating methods.

You can also coach yourself. We have already mentioned the trick of checking your skating tracks in new snow to see how long you glide and when you start to edge. Good skaters not only glide efficiently, they also push for a long period of time. If you start forcing your push, you slow down. Compare your tracks with other skaters.

Shadows are used by skiers to improve technique. With the sun at my back, I watch to see if my arms are out too far or whether I'm keeping them in tight for more power. Am I turning my whole torso in the direction I'm skating? From the side, I can see the angle of my arms when I plant my poles, whether I'm smoothly transferring weight from ski to ski.

Shadow someone else—ski behind a good skier and mimic the movements. Try to keep your glide going as long, even match up the tracks in the snow if possible. This is a great way to learn. Then, if possible, get a good skier to follow you and coach you as you ski along together.

Find a coach. Coaches that work with your kids or other racers are great sources of advice. Many ski racers coach a little and are willing to give you a few tips. A good coach has the knack of spotting things right away. Just a five minute observation and a quick comment like "Use your ankle more" can save you days of experimenting on your own.

But whether you coach yourself or work with a professional ski instructor, be a thinking skier. "Stretch your mind a bit, try new things when skating. Techniques are still evolving," says Hank Lange. Lange, an experienced ski coach and fitness consultant, demonstrated his point as he used a marathon skate on an uphill stretch, even though there were no set tracks. "Instead of poling into the slope as usual, try keeping one ski parallel and using the terrain falling away to skate. See if it works for you."

Experiment with the angle of your skating skis. Simple vector analysis from high school physics tells us that skating 45 degrees off to the side is inefficient, that the more we can decrease that angle, the more force we can direct down the track. The object is to direct as much energy as possible in a forward direction. Some experts see this as the next refinement of skating.

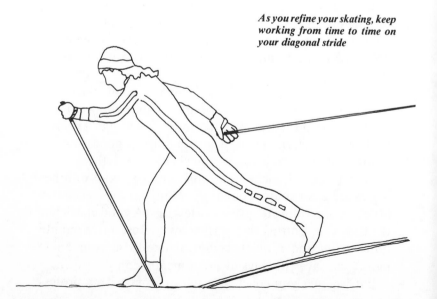

As you refine your skating, keep working from time to time on your diagonal stride

As you refine the variations of skating, don't abandon your traditional skiing altogether. For citizen racers, there are a growing number of diagonal races and all major race series, from juniors to masters, feature skating and traditional categories. "It helps your skating," explains St. Lawrence University ski coach Paul Daly, explaining why his skiers work on traditional techniques every Monday—even though they only skate in competition. "It's a nice rest for the mind and since you are using different muscles, for the body. With set tracks, it's also a good chance to work on double poling."

When we feel good about our technique, we are loose and relaxed and skiing the way we should be. It's important, as we work on new skating variations, not to get so hung up on the terms and timing that we get "paralysis by analysis." Every technique we have reviewed—offset, marathon skate, diagonal skate—uses the same skating motion. The rest is simply varying the timing of the poling and skating as well as changing body position to match the terrain and snow conditions. Looking good, each in our own style, is a nice goal in skating.

7 Training for skating

We learned in earlier chapters that it doesn't take Herculean powers to be a good ski skater, that a lot depends on smooth technique and the ability to balance. In this chapter, we will look at some ways to get in better condition to skate, and for those so inclined, to race on skis. If you are just interested in recreational skating on weekends, that's fine—you will find some ideas on how to make these outings easier and more fun. On the other hand, if you're trying to win some age group awards in citizen racing, we'll also look at more specific training that might help you do it. In any case, if you presently are doing some fast walking, running, or biking, skating will require no extra training at all. For most of us, training for skating will simply be to get in better aerobic shape. (Note: See your physician before beginning any exercise program.)

Dryland training is the term often used to describe off-season training for skiers. For serious ski racers, this usually involves a program of aerobic base building to which strength exercises are added. As the season nears, more specific training work is added. A look at a week in an elite skier's program shows how this all fits together.

Marianne Dahlmo is a star of the Norwegian Women's National Team, finishing 2nd in 1986 and 3rd in 1987 in the overall World Cup standings. Here's a glance at her August training dairy:

Monday—Roller skied without poles, practicing balance and weight shift. Ran distance and did circuit/strength exercises in the afternoon.

Tuesday—Roller skied working on skating uphill in morning (strength). Ran hard intervals in afternoon. Party in evening.

Wednesday—Easy 3 hour hike in morning, pace workout in afternoon.

Thursday—Easy roller ski (skating) in morning. Easy distance running in afternoon.

Friday—Strength workout, easy roller skiing in PM.

Saturday—Competed in swim/bike/run triathlon.

Sunday—Long running workout.

What can we, as recreational skiers, learn from this dry-land training camp routine of a world-ranked skier? First, note that there is a steady dose of aerobic endurance work through running and roller skiing. There is strength training, including roller skiing repeats up hills, and there is specific training by working on technique with roller skis. There is good variety and in spite of the intensity, some fun events.

You won't find a nine month training program in this book. As recreational skiers, regardless of our ability and drive, we don't need to focus in on skiing year-round to be a good skier. What we can do is identify some exercises and activities to help us get ready for skating on skis. Let's face it, most recreational skiers are not going to go out and run hills with ski poles twice a week all summer—we may intend to, but we won't. What we might do is run, bike, canoe, or hike. Find some things that make training fun and then get out and do them.

BUILDING AN AEROBIC BASE

The object of an off-season training program for recreational skiers is to get in shape so we can go out and skate as soon as there is snow and not be gasping for breath or hobbling around the next day. Whether we call it "getting in shape" or "building up the cardiovascular system," such a program starts with the building or maintenance of your aerobic base and the off-season is the time to get it done. There are a variety of exercise activities, none of them new, that fall into the general category of aerobic training.

Aerobic training goes by many names: base training, endurance training, or distance training. This is exercise that raises your heart rate up into the aerobic zone. If you train below this level, you aren't developing your cardiovascular system enough while if you exceed it, you develop more lactic acid in your system than can be assimilated and can lower your aerobic fitness. Some of the very successful Scandinavian ski programs stress the importance of easy aerobic workouts to build up a good aerobic base. To find your aerobic zone, first estimate your maximum heart rate. One way is to subtract your age from 220 (226 for women), so for a 47 year-old man, the approximate maximum heart rate would be 173. The aerobic zone is about 60% to 80% of this or 104 to 138. Many coaches aim at 70% as a good training level (121).

It is not easy to stay in the aerobic zone while training; we are tempted to push a bit harder, to beat the last training time by a few seconds. We need to learn to pace ourselves. One way is to notice the breathing pattern that corresponds to a given heart rate. Runner's call it the "talk test"—being able to hold a conversation while running.

Another monitoring method is to take your pulse during and after a workout. Hold your fingers up against the carotid artery in your neck, count the pulse for ten seconds and then multiply by six. You'll find that it is not always easy to do, especially once you are skiing. Heart rate monitors are a more accurate way to help gauge your training intensity. See if you can borrow one for a workout, they are light and unobtrusive.

Run some of the same trails you'll ski

So, what we want to do is train aerobically, to tailor a personal workout program to our schedule and, as the season nears, weave in some ski-related activities. This chapter will review some training equipment and routines that can be used to get ready for cross country skating.

Running

Running has been one of the best aerobic training tools for skiers for years. Most recreational skiers do some running and for some, it is the only type of exercise they bother with. I like to run trails, even some of the trails I ski on. The softer ground is easier on the legs while the rolling terrain provides a nice variety of exercise, similar to the climbs and recoveries in skiing.

During the aerobic phase of training, the trick is to keep most of your runs easy, to stay within your aerobic zone. Rest between tougher workouts and integrate other activities, such as bicycling, into the schedule. Serious skiers who run to build up an aerobic base over the summer, usually add a program of more specific running workouts as the season nears. They take their ski poles along and run up hills (sometimes called "bounding") in a skating motion. We'll look at some of these techniques later in this chapter.

Hiking

Walking has gained popularity as an aerobic workout and many, who never liked running or who cannot run without injury, now fastwalk for exercise. Walking is not only one of the safest ways to get started with an exercise program, it also is a good start toward aerobic training for skating. But, because you don't just walk on skis when skating, you have to do more than just stroll around the block; you should get your heart rate up in the exercise zone for at least 20 minutes.

Trail hiking, climbing and descending at a steady pace, is a great off-season way to train for skiing. Racers, especially those in Europe, like this as a training routine. It provides a nice variation and can be an enjoyable change from regular workouts. Hiking with ski poles, using them to climb the hills, is likewise a popular summer training method. Like walking, hiking should be fast enough to get the heart rate into the aerobic zone if we are going to use it for aerobic training.

Biking

Many recreational skiers, especially those who race, ride bicycles in the off-season. Elite skiers do a lot of biking because it is quite compatible to ski skating; it builds up the quadriceps and works the hips. There's less hammering of

Racers find bicycling an excellent preparation for skating

the legs than in running, and the routine—working hard on the climbs and recovering on the descents—is much like skiing. It is an excellent way to add long duration aerobic training to your schedule.

One out of four bikes sold these days is a mountain bike. It is easy to see why—they are fun, easy to ride, and can go anywhere about any time of the year. They are especially good for cross country ski training since, if you ride them on trails, you not only work the legs but, due to all the "honking around" you have to do while climbing, also get a good upper body workout as well. As one enthusiast explained,

Mountain bikes can give you a good upper body workout

"You need your whole body. You're constantly pushing the bike and balancing in positions that put stress on your chest and shoulder muscles. Going downhill, you really throw the bike around." Even if you are not inclined to charge up muddy hills, these 18-gear beauties are a great way to ride nearly year-round. Because you ride in a more upright position, mountain bikes are very easy for novices to master.

Water Sports

Swimming is well known for its aerobic benefits. It is also an excellent way to help develop strength and flexibility in upper body muscles. There are a couple of problems for skiers: first, swimming requires a certain skill level to get a good workout and secondly, since most serious swimming is done during the winter, it conflicts with skiing workouts. If you are a good swimmer and like to do laps, use swimming to keep muscles loose and flexible.

Paddling canoes and kayaks is a terrific way to get the upper body and the cardiovascular system ready for skiing. A lot of excellent canoe racers are also very good citizen racers. The poling motion of skating is much like that of paddling, in fact, one new ski pole design has a handle shaped like a paddle. Paddling strengthens the large abdominal muscles that are so important for good double poling. Again, canoeing and kayaking must get your heart rate into the aerobic zone. While there's nothing wrong with an easy twilight tour in a canoe, you need to be stroking right along to consider it training.

STRENGTH TRAINING

A Scandinavian definition of strength is to be able to use your muscles, in the same range of motion, many times. In other words, you want strength for endurance, not necessarily strength to lift the front end of a Volvo.

Skating, with its long poles and lateral leg push, uses some muscles that we don't normally strengthen. A good training program, even for a recreational skier, should involve some strength work to go with endurance training. This might be as simple as cutting and splitting firewood or digging and hoeing a garden or it could be more formal. Here are some options. As with endurance training, we need to find some things that we like to do and then get with it.

Arm Strengtheners

Sweden's ace skier, Gunde Svan, reportedly logs a lot of "TV time" and it all counts toward training. While watching the tube, he pulls, in a poling motion, on some surgical tubing attached to the ceiling. Just think of how much upper body strength some of us could build this way.

This type of resistive exercise is not new. Long before hi-tech exercise devices were touted in glossy mail-order catalogs and inflight magazines, nordic skiers were nailing old bicycle tubes to trees or posts and, standing as they would on skis, trained by yanking away. (Coach John Caldwell and his crew of national ski team members from southern Vermont pioneered the use of the inexpensive training aids in the late 1960's. In the lore of cross country skiing, these tubes are known as "Putney arm bands.") While bike tubes or elastic bands certainly still work to simulate poling motion, there are other devices available that are lightweight and portable. Brand names include *Exer-Genie,* the *SPORT Fit Kit* and the *Lifeline Gym.*

Look for opportunities to work on your upper body. Dr. John Ayer, a 68 year-old skier, uses his commuting time creatively. He does isometric exercises against the steering wheel and has developed other workouts which, in the interest of traffic safety, will not be detailed. The point is, he is always looking for a chance to exercise—and he's an accident-free driver to boot.

Rollerboards

The rollerboard is another homemade training device, first used by the East Germans, that has, since the mid-1970's, been part of many a serious skier's workout routine. It consists of an inclined plywood ramp, a dolly with castered wheels, and a pair of ropes. You lie or kneel on the dolly and pull yourself up the incline with the ropes. A good description of how to make a rollerboard is in Bob Woodward's book, *Cross-Country Ski Conditioning.* With a couple of sheets of plywood, some 2 X 4's, and some wheels, rope, and fasteners, you're in business.

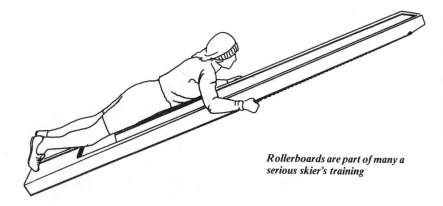

*Rollerboards are part of many a
serious skier's training*

Weight Training

Some of the best weight training for skiers is done without
weights—the rollerboard is a good example. Some coaches
believe that you should move your body instead of moving
weights or pulleys. Perform the repetitions quickly, simu-
lating the action you are going to perform. Pullups, situps,
pushups, and using a rollerboard are the weight routine of
many a good skier.

There's a new generation of training equipment now
available to recreational skiers for strength training. The
exercise machines, Nautilus and Universal, for instance, are,
after a little instruction, easy to use and are an excellent way
to condition for skating. Nearly all stations are helpful, in
fact most coaches suggest that you use them all and not get
too specific. The adductor/abductor machines are good for
strengthening the skating muscles while the Super Pullover
machine is especially helpful for double poling.

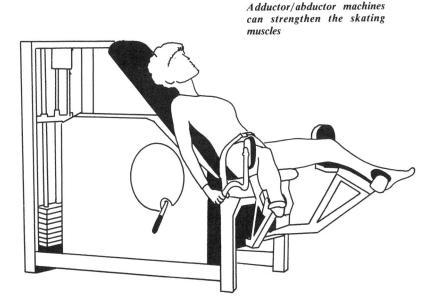

Adductor/abductor machines can strengthen the skating muscles

If you want to work with free weights, get some help from an experienced lifter or coach. Use moderate amounts of weight and learn the right way to do an exercise. Squats, done properly, are a good use of free weights in general conditioning for skaters. Bench presses, bent rows, and abdominal exercises are also good routines for skating. Remember your goal in weight training. You're not interested in becoming a bodybuilder, you want to work on flexibility and strength. As instructors will tell you, strength training should be done two or three times a week at the most.

Nordic Simulators

Nordic simulators are widely advertised devices that incorporate the aerobic benefits of cross country skiing into your home gym. They tend to be more expensive than most exercise bicycles or rowing machines and like any training equipment, some are used routinely while others gather dust in the basement. For skating, the major benefit is the general endurance training you can pick up and the upper body exercise from the poling action.

The two that are cited as being most specific to cross country skiing are Nordic Track and Fitness Master. Both offer "jar-less" aerobic exercise and are generally considered to be effective for conditioning. Make sure that you'll use one before making such a major investment. Sign up for a trial membership at a fitness club that has one and see if you like the routine. Look for new skating-oriented trainers on the market from Scandinavia.

SKATING-SPECIFIC TRAINING

The component of training that marks the serious skier is specificity—doing specific routines that are directly applicable for ski-skating. Specific exercises work the muscles in the same way they will be used to skate. Done to build strength and quickness and to prevent injuries, these routines are often added to the training program as the ski season nears. For example, use the late spring and summer to build aerobic endurance through a program of running and biking. As fall approaches, add some strength work, perhaps Nautilus workouts a couple times a week. Then, layer on specific training to hone your general conditioning toward skiing. Here are a few suggestions.

Fall Running Routines

Skating on skis uses muscles in the thighs that are not used in running; you direct pressure straight down the inside of the leg to the ski. This lateral movement works the abductor muscles as well as the external rotators of the hip. You also use muscles in the arms, shoulders and abdomen as you

Ski Striding — running hills with poles, is a common training method

skate with long poles. You'll probably feel some soreness in these areas after your first few outings on snow.

There are a number of things that you can incorporate into a running program to help train for skating. The easiest is to run with ski poles. Ski coach Hank Lange says, "You can get off the roads and run with poles in the woods. The varying terrain is a nice break. I run with my poles up hills or sometimes I just hike. It not only gives a whole new perspective on running, it also benefits both running and skiing."

The trick to training with poles is to run naturally and just gently plant the pole when it is ready, about every other stride. I find that my ski poles comes down about every two strides—in other words, my right pole strikes once for every two strikes of my right foot. If it doesn't work out quite like that, it is no big deal, the idea is to let your arms swing normally, just as you will do when you ski. You will find that it is more tiring than straight running, even though the ski poles are light. Run your normal routes at your normal pace, or at first, even a little slower. Try not to concentrate on the poles, just let them come down naturally. After a few tries, your self-consciousness will vanish.

Most skiers concentrate on the hills when using poles; some bound up the hill using the staggered double pole just as in skating. If you go out with poles to run hills in the fall, instead of going straight up a hill, run diagonally back and forth across the slopes, bounding off the inner leg muscles. With your poles, try to lift yourself up the hill with each pole plant, using your arms to help propel you up the hill. The feeling will be very much like the thrust you get from your poles while skating.

Slideboards

First used by speed skaters, slideboards are also used by some ski racers to train for skating. Since they are cheap to build, you might consider adding one to your training program. Slideboards are simply a six to eight foot sheet of formica counter top (look in your discount lumber houses or talk to contractors who renovate kitchens) with padded sidewalls. Slide some wool socks over your shoes and you are in business. You push off with one leg, just like in skating, and slide to the opposite side of the board on your other foot. Some racers find that a spray can of furniture polish works better than talcum powder to keep the glide going. Practice in front of a mirror so that you can check your technique. Some skiers practice with ankle weights to make the workout a little tougher, and shorter. Like riding a stationary bike, skating on a slideboard, in spite of its training benefits, can get old pretty fast. Which is why roller skis and training skates are popular—they are fun.

Slideboards simulate the action of skating on snow

Roller Skis/Skateblades

For every ski racer who uses roller skis for skate training, there's another who swears by training skates. If you get serious about skating, you may find yourself looking at a pair of one or the other.

Before we go further, forget whatever you've heard about picking up bad habits using these trainers. So what if you start lifting your non-skating leg too high or developing a little "dipsy-doodle" in your skate? The idea is to have fun while you train. Any habits will work themselves out once you are on snow.

Roller skis have been used by cross country skiers for many years. They are an excellent training device, the closest thing to actual skiing. Long roller skis are designed for diagonal stride and double poling. These older rollers have a ratchet arrangement that allows you to push off for the diagonal stride. Use them for diagonal stride on the uphills and for double poling on the flats. Quite a few skiers have cut them short for skating.

Roller skis allow you to train for diagonal stride and skating

If you are going to purchase roller equipment, buy a
system that allows you to skate. The new roller skis are light
and short and designed for skating. Some have ratchets so
that they can be used for diagonal striding as well. They are
not cheap, costing from $175 to $225. There also is a maintenance cost—the soft wheels wear very fast due to the skating
motion. Switch skis each time you train to help balance wear.

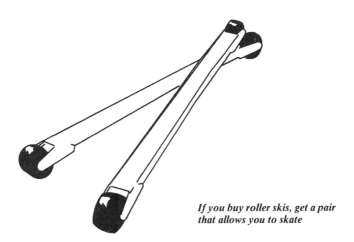

*If you buy roller skis, get a pair
that allows you to skate*

Training skates, used by speed skaters and hockey players
as well, are popular with many competitive skiers. They are
less expensive (prices range from $100 to $135). Slower
wheels are available which give you a much better workout
(the others are too fast to have much training effect), and
most models have a heel braking system. As one skier told
me, "This can't be training. It's too much fun."

You can use your regular ski poles for roller skiing but
should replace the basket and the tip with a unit designed for
the roads. Roller ferrules cost about $10 and have a hard
carbide tip better suited for asphalt.

Roller skiing can be dangerous, especially if your balance is not too good. Many motorists are not used to seeing a skier skating down the road, so skate defensively. Here are some safety guidelines for roller skiing/skateblading:

1. Stay off the roads altogether until you feel proficient at skating. Use a high school, factory, or church parking lot. Go there during off-hours to practice. Once you are comfortable, find some hills to practice on.
2. Do not roller ski downhill—there's no training gained and the risks of injury are obvious. It is safer and more beneficial to take off the skis and jog down, then ski back up.
3. Wear a fluorescent vest and put markings on your poles.
4. Wear a biking helmet and other gear such as gloves. Many skiers wear knee and elbow pads. "Road rash" is no fun.
5. Stay off busy roads. Look for back roads with little traffic and smooth surfaces. When a car approaches, double pole to use less of the road.
6. Establish a routine so that drivers get used to seeing you careening down the road.

I took my first fall on roller skis wearing just a T-shirt and shorts. In trying to switch sides with my poling, I planted a pole right between my legs. Left knee hit, left elbow, and then, left temple. It was scary—that asphalt was hard. Fortunately, no cars were around and all I got were bruises and a ringing headache—and a good lesson.

Roller skiing is one of the best ways to insure that you'll be starting off ski season in fine shape. Not only do you get a very specific workout, you also build strength as well as endurance. You also develop your balance long before the snow arrives so that when it does, you can get out and ride that flat ski.

Roller skis/skates are fun but for some, they may be too much fun and not enough work. Some physiological studies of elite skiers have shown a drop in overall oxygen uptake efficiency, a decrease attributed to relying too much on roller training. You will find that, once you are secure with your balance, skating on rollers is quite easy on the flats. If you want to work harder, double pole the flats and do your skating on the uphills. This is more of a potential problem for serious racers; for recreational skaters, just getting out and getting some good total body exercise in the fresh air, and having fun while doing it, is worth the price of the equipment.

Whether you run, swim, or roller ski, look for ways to fit your training routines into your daily routine. Dick Richards, an accomplished citizen racer from upstate New York, runs a laboratory for a hospital. He also runs up the steps of the adjoining parking garage, jogging back down the ramps to ease the pounding on his legs. During one of his first sessions, the security staff alerted to a "weirdo" in the garage, chased him. Now he checks in with them and folks are getting used to "that skier in the garage."

So pull on your pulley, slide on your slideboard—do your exercise thing. It will make your skating just that much more fun once you hit the snow.

8 Skating citizen races

A book on skating would not be complete without a section on racing because skating and racing are partners—once you learn to skate you very well may want to try a low key race. If you are already racing, you know the benefits of skating; there's no faster way to travel on cross country skis. But, just as you can get a lot of enjoyment from cross country skiing without ever skating, so can you also enjoy skating without ever entering a race. It is up to you. Citizen ski racing is an option open to anyone, from 8 to 80, who owns a pair of skis. Many first-timer racers are surprised at how much they like it.

Citizen races, often called loppets in Canada, come in a variety of lengths and levels of difficulty. Some are low key events put on by a local group and are similar to the many 10K road runs or bikeathons that take place each year. Others are national events, attracting hundreds or thousands of skiers of all abilities. Regardless of their makeup, ski races can be a great way to test skating techniques and, at the same time, learn from others. Cross country ski racing is no longer for just a few diehards in knickers and wooden skis, it is gaining more attention and more participants. No longer do you have to be a master of waxing or have started racing as a child—

skating is a great equalizer. Skating has drawn many new competitors from the ranks of runners, bikers, and canoeists.

There is a place for everyone in citizen races. Serious racers skate off at the front of the pack while novices take their time at the back. There is a wide mix of age and ability, and it's this makeup that can make racing a family and social affair.

There's a place for everyone in citizen races

But don't we get enough competition in our daily lives, do we need to go out and skate madly in a race? That is the feeling of some skiers—they shun the race scene, enjoying their sport without feeling the need to compete. Cross country skiing appeals to many because of the solitude, the serenity of the snowy woods, the chance to get away from the crowd. At the same time, many skiers who love the solitude also love to try a few races. They like the challenge of completing a long marathon ski race, of bettering a time from a previous year, or of beating a friend across the finish line.

PICKING A RACE TO SKATE

There are two basic types of cross country races: the open race and the citizen race. Open races are aimed at the competitive skier and may be strictly for one particular age group—for instance, junior skiers. It is not the place for recreational skiers to try their legs at skating. These races do offer a great chance to watch good cross country skiers in action, to see the techniques they use. It is fun, and educational, to watch the ease with which they fly down the course and how they shift skating gears going uphill.

The standard distance for citizen races is 15K for men and 10K for women, although the distances range from under 10K to over 50K. There are many citizen races that have an unusual distance, necessitated by the local course layout. Citizen races usually have a mass start, where hundreds of skis and ski poles begin moving at once. Age group awards are usually in ten year increments for male and female.

Cross country ski races are not widely publicized. Newcomers to racing are surprised to find out just how many races there are in an area during the winter. To learn more about them, join a nordic ski club if you have one locally. Ski club newsletters often list local races, some of the non-sanctioned events that are not on other schedules. Some clubs have race "hot lines" with recorded messages about upcoming events. One of the best ways to learn about future races is to ask other skiers after a race—you'll hear about some races you didn't know existed. For years, the ski race circuit was publicized by grapevine and it still pays to be tied into a network. Then when an event's date is changed to the following week due to lack of snow, you won't be driving hours to get to a rescheduled race.

Make sure that skating is allowed at the race you pick. Most citizen races allow both skating and traditional techniques but there are some events limited to diagonal stride. That's nice to know before you show up ready to race with glide-waxed skis. For skating, the course should be packed and wide enough to handle skaters—avoid the narrow tree-lined courses with a lot of uphill and descents. Some of the big marathon events which are covered later in this chapter offer a good chance to try a skating race. Some have preparatory races a few weeks ahead of the big event. Since the organizers of these races are used to skaters, the course and the snow preparation should be good for skating.

GETTING READY TO RACE

Ski races, whether a local winter carnival race or a big name event, have a pre-race atmosphere of pent-up energy. Nervous skiers are looking for the porta-potties while last minute arrivals are trying to get registered. Get to a race in plenty of time—you not only have to get yourself ready to go but also your equipment. Local race organizers are often neophytes, and registration may be painfully slow. The hubbub is compounded as racers try to wax, change into clothing, and stay warm before the race.

It is fun to people-watch at citizen races. Skiers race in everything from plaid hunting coats (with the license still pinned on the back) to wildly-colored form-fitting racing suits. You may see some wooden skis, and you're sure to see about every skating ski on the market. But don't be fooled by appearances: some who shun glitzy racing equipment are very good skiers—you may see some excellent skating done on old equipment.

During your first skating races, you may, like many of us, hear the siren call of kick wax. "Put a little Extra Blue under the foot, it'll help you up the hills," the pre-race voices say. Well, carry some kick wax for insurance or ease of mind but if you've been skating on glide-waxed skis up to now, don't backslide. You will regret it the minute you try to glide.

On the other hand, if you don't know the course, don't assume that you can skate the whole thing. Most races present no problems, but some do. I found that out the hard way at a race at a local county park. We skated the first couple of miles fine, and I felt I was off to a great race. But, by the five mile mark, we were down to one snowmobile trail with snow banks that prevented skating. Things began going downhill for me as the course climbed uphill. (Pun intended) I was in deep trouble, trying to double pole or do a narrow herringbone as more and more skiers caught up with me and passed, all diagonal striding. Oh, my kingdom for a tin of kick wax! I started begging as they passed but no one was carrying any, or admitted to it. One guy said, "I never use it, these are no-wax skis." The ultimate putdown to a skater. Finally a kind soul came by with a fanny pack and after a quick daub of grip wax on each ski, I was climbing. It was a good lesson in either knowing the condition of the whole race course beforehand or being prepared to diagonal stride.

If you are new to racing, be careful about wearing too much clothing. You will be surprised at how warm you get once you get moving and how much fluid you lose. Take your lead from other racers. Carry a light fanny pack with a light shell or extra hat in it—you will never notice the extra weight. You'll see many racers carrying a water bottle in a belt pack—a great idea for longer races.

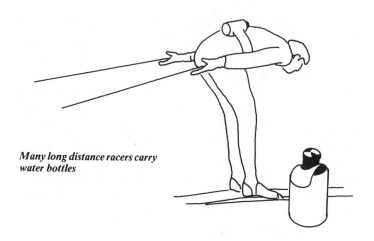

Many long distance racers carry water bottles

Warm up on skis before the race to check the conditions and once your muscles are warm, do some stretching. There often is not enough water available at the start of a race so bring your own just to be sure and drink several glasses, up to 32 ounces, in the hour before the race. You should be all set with the preparation of your skis but you may want to brush them or wax the sidewalls, just for a last minute tuneup. Stay warm just before the race by jogging in place and if it is frigid, wait as long as you can to shed your warmup clothing.

SURVIVING THE START

Mass starts at skating races are friendly chaos as long poles and short skis get up close and personal. Many races, trying to avoid interference problems, ban skating in the first kilometer. If you have only glide wax on, be ready to double pole. I love mass starts. It is an unforgettable experience to look up ahead at the double poling skiers, each reaching up and hunching over, up and down, looking much like a herd of stampeding kangaroos. Then the skating starts and the heads stay more upright.

Mass starts at skating races can be "friendly chaos"

Until you have raced a while, it will be a little hard to seed yourself, not knowing how fast you'll ski. Get in place and sort of spread out a bit, sticking your poles in on each side, staking out a claim. You'll find that too many people line up too far in front and nearly get trampled in the first rush. Take it easy, keep your balance, be courteous, and remember that there's a lot of race ahead. The race will soon settle down as skiers find their own pace.

SKATING THE RACE

Racing tests your skating ability in many ways. Not only does a citizen race measure how fast you can ski a certain distance, it also finds out if you can do it without getting too tangled up with other skiers. Skating, with its long poles and long glides, takes up a lot of room, and with just glide wax on, it's not always easy to just step aside and let someone pass. Learning to blend in with other skaters is a lesson racers have to learn from experience.

Ever try to get by a big truck that was hogging the white line? Skating takes up so much space that it often takes some common courtesy to let someone pass. In a recent race, a young college racer came up behind me and said, "On your left." I moved over, said, "You've got it," and promptly planted my left ski pole right between his legs. Fortunately, he kept his balance and raced off to the echo of my panted apologies.

There is a lot of passing, especially during the first part of the race. Some skiers skate up hills better than others, some are better on the flats, others ski in spurts and then slow down. Most people passing are polite, saying or yelling "track" or "on the left" to let you know that they want to pass. On most courses, if you are skating, ski in the left lane if it is not tracked and then get to the right as skiers come up behind you. Take your time changing tracks, this is no time to fall.

The pileups, especially back in the pack, often come at the first big downhill. Try to maintain a safe distance behind the person in front, and hope that everyone stays upright. After you get to the bottom, keep double poling—it is easy to get plowed into by someone from behind and get knocked down—after you have made it down safely. If you fall, get your skis and poles out of the track. Roll over to the side and wait for a good opening before starting out again.

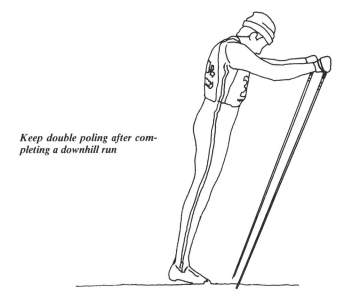

Keep double poling after completing a downhill run

Climbs are where it can get frustrating as a skater. If you are back with less competent skiers, it is easy to get bogged down and lose your momentum because of the skiers ahead. You may have to herringbone hills that you could normally handle by skating just because of the slowpokes ahead. Conversely, you may have better climbers breathing down your neck as you labor up in a diagonal skate. The more you race, the less you'll worry about these situations. If there's no room to pass, do it once you crest the hill. Uphills tend to separate the weak skaters from the better ones—and if you've got your offset skate down, you'll find that hills are where you can pick up ground. Keep your cool and ski loosely, after all this is supposed to be fun.

The frustration of passing in skating might have been epitomized in the 1987 World Championship women's relay race when a Swedish skier, who had just finished her leg of the race and was watching her teammate try to pass a skier who would not yield the track, rapped the offender, Italian racer Elena Deseri, on the head and shoulders with a ski pole. Courtesy goes a long way in solving the problems of interference, be it at the local loppet or on the World Cup circuit.

As the race goes on, you can expect to have any set tracks pretty well chewed up by the racers ahead, especially where the course is narrow. Most race courses are set for skating on the left and for diagonal striding on the right. Use the tracks for double poling and marathon skating to give your V-skating muscles a break. It is a nice relaxation for the ankles as well.

Ski racing is a great place to work on technique and to learn to ski efficiently. John Burton, a 1952 Olympic team racer, is a self-taught skier. An accomplished skier in the 60-64 Masters age group, he likes to learn from others. "I like to watch the skiers up ahead," he says. "Some are smooth, some are rough. I learn a lot from observation." Do

*Mimic other racers during a
race — learn from them*

the same, ski behind other skaters in the race, matching them stride for stride. Mimic the good ones and skate past the others. Relax, work on keeping a flat ski, don't grip your poles tightly, and work on switching double poling from side to side every so often.

Drink water in the race whenever you can. Many shorter races don't have water stops but if they do, grab a drink— even though the temperature is cold, you need the fluids. In marathons, you can lose up to 13 pounds of water and you have to start replacing that water before you get thirsty. Expect to receive lukewarm water or a sweet sports drink such as GatorAid or ERG, but don't experiment: pass up the sweet sticky liquids unless you are sure that your stomach can handle it—drink water if it is available. It is more readily absorbed by your system.

As the race progresses and you tire, you may find yourself edging your skis too soon or not getting up and over your poles. The simplest downhill can present problems late in the race. Concentrate on technique and try to ski smoothly. As you approach the finish, avoid last minute sprints—this is no time to plant a pole inside a ski and put on a show for the finish line folks.

SKATING A MARATHON

Completing a ski marathon, all 50 kilometers of it, is a goal that draws thousands of skiers to citizen races across North America. A new goal for many of these enthusiasts is not only to ski, but to skate a complete marathon. Each year, more and more recreational skiers accomplish that goal and in doing so, usually take minutes or hours off their marathon times.

Ski marathons come in many configurations—some are local loppets with attendance in the hundreds while others are international affairs with thousands of entrants. A common length is 50 to 55 kilometers. Nearly all marathons have a shorter race option, quite often 25 K, which may be the best bet for your first long skating race.

Pre-race preparation for a marathon is not unlike a shorter race except that you may want to do some carbohydrate loading the night before the race—a spaghetti dinner fills the bill for many skiers. It's going to be a long time on skis for you so start race day with a wholesome breakfast. For the race, some marathon skiers carry some snacks such as orange slices, figs, or granola bars in a pocket or pouch. I like to reach in and treat myself after a tough hill or another 5 kilometers skied. As mentioned before, even though liquids are available at feeding stations, the new water bottle carriers, where the plastic bottle rides in the small of the back, are very popular with long distance skiers.

Most large marathons have a mass start by waves, with

the faster skiers starting first. Because there are more skiers than at shorter races, marathon starts can be quite frenetic as skaters and diagonal striders try to get going. People tend to forget that they have 31 miles ahead. It will take several kilometers for things to calm down, and in big races, you'll have to deal with congestion during the whole race. This clashing of skis and poles brings out the worst in some people, but in general, the spirit is good. I take a general attitude of "I won't trip you and please don't trip me" and then if we get tangled up, just laugh and get going again.

Smart skiers ski a steady pace, trying hard to save their energy for the second half of the race. I figure that I have a certain reservoir of energy and every hill I take too fast early on draws down the tank too fast and I'll be "running on empty" if I don't use my head. When you get tired, "latent awkwardness" seems to come out in full force. You find that instead of being up over the ski in a nice skate, you're hunched over, not committing properly to either ski. You may be skiing on the inside edge instead of keeping the ski flat. Your whole ski operating system needs rebooting—you need to smooth things out. There are a number of strategies to use: stay away from energy-depleting techniques like the V-2 (poling with every skate), change techniques continually (double pole on one side for 20 strokes, then switch to the other, for example), and transition early to a diagonal skate on the uphills. To save energy, use the tracks—let your skating muscles and your ankles relax for a while as you double pole. In some conditions such as soft snow, the skating section of the trail will be chewed up and slow from all the preceding skiers but the track may be glazed and a lot faster.

You never know what you'll find to drink at feeding stations during a marathon. There may be warm ERG, Gatorade, cocoa, or some fruit concoction. Drink water if you can and save any sugary drinks until later in the race.

You need to eat during a long race to help replace the energy you are expending over the four hours plus you're skiing. Foods include cookies, banana bread, oranges, and chocolate bars. Grab some of the goodies, they'll help you skate those last few kilometers.

The second half of the race, especially the last 15 kilometers, becomes a case of concentrating and trying to ski as efficiently as possible. Conversations slacken as skiers focus on their primary tasks, to keep the skating going and to finish the marathon. As you tire, you may want to shift down a skating gear by diagonal skating hills that earlier you could climb with the V-1 offset.

About now you may start thinking about kick wax as you feel your skating muscles complain. During my first skating marathon, I stopped at about the 40K mark, put on some grip wax, and immediately found that I just couldn't diagonal stride after having skated that distance—my tired muscles just wouldn't respond to a new technique. Of course, when I switched back to skating I found my glide was being killed by the grip wax. I then vowed to henceforth stick with glide wax regardless of what my legs were telling me.

Marathons are not the agonizing affairs that road running marathons can be. While there's some stiffness the next day, you should be ready to ski right away if you've paced yourself. Many citizen racers complete several marathons in a season and some ski one nearly every weekend. As thousands of skiers have learned, skiing 30 to 35 miles is well within the ability of most skiers. Skating the distance takes more ability but is being accomplished by more and more recreational skiers. In huge races like the American Birkebeiner, all the top skiers are skating and more and more of those in the following waves also skate.

There are marathons scattered across North America. Some of the best in the U.S. comprise the Leaf Great

American Ski Chase, a series of eight races at locations across the country. The Canadian Ski Odyssey consists of eight events spread from New Brunswick to British Columbia. For skiers who like to combine travel with marathoning, the Worldloppet international series, which draws up to 80,000 skiers a year, is composed of 11 of the most famous ski marathons in the world.

Whether you travel to another country or sign up for a local marathon, skating 50 kilometers is within your reach. If you train for the race, set an easy pace, take plenty of food and liquids along the way, and enjoy the camaraderie and competition, you'll be surprised at how much fun it is, and how spry you feel the next day.

Skating has brought a lot of new skiers into ski racing. It is surprising to find that some of the top finishers in local races may have only been skiing for several years. Granted, they are usually talented runners, bikers, canoeists, or alpine skiers, but skating has enabled them to get fast and competitive with very little experience. Further back in the list of finishers, there are many average skiers who have lowered their race times significantly by learning to skate. If you haven't tried citizen racing, give it a try—it can be a great way to spend a winter Saturday morning. Even if you don't win a ribbon or medal, you'll pick up some pointers and come home with a better appreciation for skating on skis.

GLOSSARY

Aerobic   Skiing "with oxygen" at a pace within the training heart rate.

Aerobic capacity   The ability to supply oxygen to the muscle tissues.

Anaerobic   Skiing "without oxygen." Also called oxygen debt.

Anaerobic Threshold   A borderline, about 85% of the maximum heart rate.

Bail   The metal piece that clamps over a boot to hold it to the ski.

Basket   The device attached to the bottom of the ski pole to keep the pole from sinking into the snow.

Biathlon   A rapidly growing sport which combines marksmanship and cross country skiing.

Bill Koch Ski League   The youth program of the U.S. Ski Association.

Binder wax   Also called base wax, it is used to make grip wax wear longer.

Biomechanics   Using the science of mechanics to study physiological movements.

Bounding   Running, usually uphill, using bounding motions to simulate diagonal stride or skating.

Camber   The arch built into skis to support the skier's weight while allowing the ski to glide.

Carbo loading   A controversial technique of depleting oxygen and then increasing carbohydrate intake. Most skiers/runners skip the depletion stage.

Carbon fiber   A material used in ski pole shafts and skis.

CCC   Cross Country Canada, an arm of the Canadian Ski Association.

Chair dip   A dip down between two chairs. Used to strengthen the arm muscles and shoulder girdle.

Christie   A skidding turn on both uphill ski edges.

Citizen race   A ski race for everyone. Called a loppet in Canada.

Cork   A block of cork (often synthetic) that is used to polish grip wax.

Delamination   The splitting of fiberglass skis, often at the tails.

Diagonal Stride   The classic cross country technique, similar to running, where the arm and opposite leg swing forward together.

Double camber   The center section of skis where the camber is stiffer.

Double pole   Propelling oneself forward with both poles. An important technique for any skier, not just racers.

F.I.S.   Federation International de Ski, the international governing body for skiing.

Fall line   Shortest line up or down the hill.

Fannypack   A beltlike pack, also called a bumbag.

Fartlek   A training method familiar to runners. Means "speed play" and involves changing speeds during a workout.

Fast-twitch fibers   Muscle fibers that release glycogen rapidly. Skiers/runners with good speed have a high percentage.

Feed   A drink containing sugar and salts such as ERG.

Flat ski   Skiing with the surface flat on the snow. Important in skating.

Flex   How easily a ski or ski pole bends.

Gaiters   Waterproof cuffs used to keep snow out of ski boots.

Glide wax   A hard wax used on the glide zone for diagonal stride and on the whole ski base for skating.

Glycogen   The substance stored in muscles and used up in long races.

Grip   The thrust onto the snow that propels a skier forward in the diagonal stride. Also called kick.

Hard wax   Solid grip wax, such as green, used for new snow.

Heart monitor   A training device strapped across the chest which determines heart rate. Usually has a wristwatch display.

Heel plate   A plate or disk with ridges to keep ski boot heel in place when weight is on the ski.

Herringbone   A "V-walking" movement used to climb steep hills.

Hypothermia   A decrease in body temperature caused by exposure. A potentially serious problem for skiers and runners.

Imagery   A "psyching" technique used to get ready to compete.

Interval training   Alternating hard exercise with recovery periods.

Jackrabbit Ski League   Canada's ski program for youth.

Kick   See Grip.

Kick Turn   A method of reversing direction when standing still.

Kicker   A grip wax applied in the wax pocket of the ski.

Kinesthetic sense   Awareness of what is happening to the body.

Klister   A sticky liquid wax used when there is refrozen snow.

Knickers   Knee length ski pants, used with long socks.

Lactic acid   The substance generated at a rate faster than the body can assimilate when skiers/runners go into oxygen debt.

Layering   Dressing for skiing in layers, usually three. (Wicking, insulation, protection.)

Loppet   A "people's race." Called a citizen race in the U.S.

Marathon skate   A skating motion used with prepared tracks.

Masters   Skiers who are over age 30.

Max oxygen uptake   A measure of the capacity of the oxygen system.

Mohair   A hairy material used in strips to provide grip on some no-wax skis.

Negative base   A patterned waxless base cut into the ski.

Nordic combined   An event combining ski jumping and cross country racing.

Nordic norm   The standard system used for the 75mm boot/binding system.

No-wax skis   Skis that get their grip from a patterned bottom, chemical base, or some other non-wax system.

Offset skating   Also called staggered poling, it has become the primary skating technique. Poles are planted sequentially.

One-skate   A skating method for the flats and gradual uphills. Double poling thrust on each skate. Requires good balance.

Orienteering   Navigation with map and compass to preselected points.

Overboots   Light covers that pull over ski boots. Used in cold or wet conditions, especially over thin racing boots.

Oxygen debt   Going past the anaerobic threshold in exertion.

P-tex   A polyethylene base material, variations of which are used on ski bases.

P-tex candle   A stick of plastic which is melted to repair scratches and gouges on ski bases.

Paper test   A method of evaluating camber/stiffness of skis in relation to a skier's weight and ability.

Pine tar   A black gooey substance that is used to prepare the base of wooden skis.

Plyometrics   Lengthening a muscle (stretching it) before it contracts. The basis of some current skating training methods.

Positive Base   A patterned base where the grip surface protrudes from the base.

Pulk   A sled pulled by a skier to move kids or provisions.

Pulley   A simple way to strengthen arms for poling. Most have variable resistance.

Rilling   Cutting fine ridges in the base of the ski to reduce the suction of wet snow. Done with a file or a special tool.

Roller skis   Short wheeled skis used to practice in off-season.

Rollerboard   A "do-it-yourself" training device for building upper body strength.

Shovel   The part of the ski tip that turns upward.

Sidecut   The reduction in ski width in the midsection that aids turning.

Sideslip   Sliding downhill sideways with control.

Siitonen technique   Another name for marathon skating, after Pauli Siitonen, the inventor of the technique.

Skate turn   A turn where the skier skates off a weighted ski.

Ski striding   Running or walking, often with ski poles.

Skins   Long mohair strips that are stuck or strapped to skis to climb. Used primarily in mountaineering skiing.

Slideboard   A training system used by speed skaters as well as some skiers. Often a formica countertop with padded sidewalls.

Slow-twitch fibers   Muscle fibers which utilize glycogen efficiently during long duration exercise.

Snowplow   Also called wedge. A slowing-down maneuver with tips together and ski tails spread apart.

Specificity   Training aimed at developing skills and muscles for a particular sport.

Step turn   A turn where the ski tips are picked up and moved, one at a time, in a new direction.

Stroke volume   The volume of blood pumped by a ventricle of the heart per beat.

Structure   The process of putting grooves in the ski base to match snow conditions.

Telemark   A skiing method featuring turns with flexed knees and the outside ski ahead of the inside ski.

Training effect   The exercise level needed to derive benefits, usually 60 to 70% of maximum heart rate.

Training skates   A popular type of dryland skating equipment. Plastic molded hockey skates with 3 to 5 two-inch wheels.

Transition snow   Snow at the freeze/thaw temperature zone.

Traverse   To ski across the hill at an angle to the fall line.

Triathlon   A winter event combining running, skiing, and biking. Sometimes ice skating or other events are substituted.

Tuck   A crouching downhill position used to cut wind resistance.

Two-wax system   A simplified grip wax system with one wax for dry snow and one wax for wet snow.

USSA   United States Ski Association

V-skate   The skating herringbone that forms the basis of most skating methods.

Wax pocket   The section of the ski base marked for grip wax.

Wedge   See Snowplow.

BIBLIOGRAPHY

BOOKS

Caldwell, John. *The Cross-Country Ski Book.* Brattleboro, VT: Stephen Green Press, 1985.
Now in its seventh edition, this is a good basic manual for all aspects of cross country skiing.

Caldwell, John and Brady, Michael. *Citizen Racing.* Seattle, WA: The Mountaineers, 1982.
A complete look at racing from two good writers. Excellent photographs of technique.

Cross Country Canada. *The National Guide to Loppet Skiing.* Prepared by Anton Scheier. Canada, 1985.
A technical guide written by Canadian experts on all aspects of loppet/citizen racing. Excellent drawing of skating techniques.

Hall, Marty. *One Stride Ahead.* Tulsa, OK: Winchester Press, 1981.
A good technical book for runners interested in racing. Hall, former U.S. and current Canadian ski team coach, covers all aspects of ski prep, waxing, training, and racing.

Woodward, Bob. *Cross-Country Ski Conditioning.* Chicago, IL: Contemporary Books, 1981.
A practical look at training for skiing. Good section on rollerboard construction. Aimed at citizen racers.

PERIODICALS

Cross Country Skier
A glossy look at what is happening in equipment, techniques, and places to ski. Published five times a year.

CCC Newsletter
Updates from the National Office of Cross Country Canada covering both recreational and competitive cross country skiing. 6 issues a year.

The Master Skier
A tabloid presentation of topics for skiers over age 30. Features on technique and skier profiles. 4 issues a season.

Nordic West
Competition and touring articles for skiers in western U.S. and Canada.

Ski Racing News
The latest in results as well as articles on all major ski racing events. If you are interested in following World Cup or national nordic competition results, you'll find them here. Twenty issues a year.

Wisconsin Silent Sports
A monthly magazine which covers many recreational and competitive subjects. Thorough cross country skiing coverage for mid-west skiers.

VIDEOS

Cross Country Ski Skating
A four part series issued by the National Collegiate Ski Association. Clear description of double poling, marathon skating, and V-skating. Good points on error corrections and drills.

INDEX

ORDER FORM

Post Office Box 7067-AA
Syracuse, NY 13261

Please send me the following books by Dick Mansfield:

———— copies of *Skating On Skis*   @ $ 9.95 each

———— copies of *Runner's Guide To
      Cross Country Skiing*   @ $10.95 each

I understand that I may return any books for a full refund if not satisfied.

Name: _____

Address: _____

_____ Zip: _____

New York residents: please add 7% sales tax.
Shipping: Add $1.00 for the first book and .25 for each additional book.

ORDER FORM

Post Office Box 7067-AA
Syracuse, NY 13261

Please send me the following books by Dick Mansfield:

_____ copies of *Skating On Skis*   @ $ 9.95 each

_____ copies of *Runner's Guide To*
      Cross Country Skiing   @ $10.95 each

I understand that I may return any books for a full refund if not satisfied.

Name: _____

Address: _____

_____ Zip: _____

New York residents: please add 7% sales tax.
Shipping: Add $1.00 for the first book and .25 for each additional book.